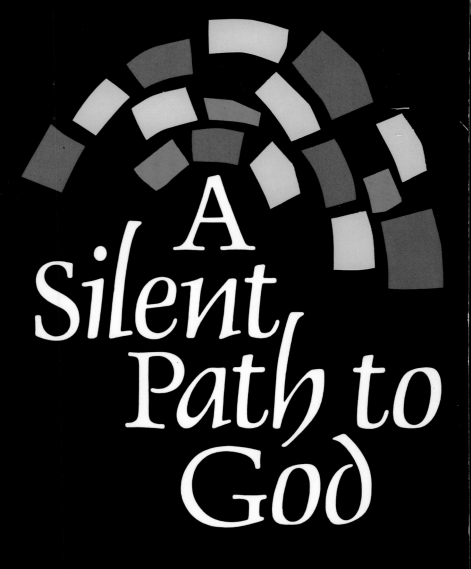

A Silent Path to God

James E. Griffiss

A Silent Path to God

William J. Spaid

A Silent Path
to God

James E. Griffiss (signature)

JAMES E. GRIFFISS

FORTRESS PRESS
Philadelphia

Biblical quotations:
From The New English Bible. © The Delegates of the Oxford University Press
and The Syndics of the Cambridge University Press 1961, 1970. Reprinted by
permission.

The quotation on pages 42–43 from *From Glory to Glory: Texts from Gregory
of Nyssa's Mystical Writings,* translated and edited by Herbert Musurillo, is
used by permission of Charles Scribner's Sons.

Library of Congress Cataloging in Publication Data

Griffiss, James E   1928–
  A silent path to God.

  Includes bibliographical references.
  1. Prayer.   2. Jesus Christ—Temptation—
Meditations.   I. Title.
BV210.2.G744   264'.1   79–8903
ISBN 0-8006-1384-8

8024J79   Printed in the United States of America   1–1384

*For my mother
and
in memory of my father*

Contents

Preface

For a theologian to write about the life of prayer and the discipline of ascetical theology requires these days a considerable degree of courage and not a little presumption. It was not always so, of course. One has only to think of the great theologians of the past in order to realize that no one can be a theologian without being a person of prayer or a person concerned with the discipline of the spiritual life. Many of the greatest treatises on the spiritual life have come from those who were engaged in the highly intellectual task of theological reflection. The problem, and the reason why both courage and presumption on the part of the theologian are required today, is that for so long there has been a great gulf between the intellectual study of theology and the ascetical discipline. Those who write well on ascetical theology do not always consider themselves to be theologians, because they see themselves creating an ascetical theology out of the work of a particular theologian or theological tradition. And the number of writings by theologians specifically dealing with ascetical discipline is very limited. There are, I believe, two reasons for the gulf between the intellectual formulation of Christian faith and the discipline of the life of prayer. The first is historical. There has developed in recent centuries a compartmentalization of disciplines in every field, which makes it difficult for a person to move out of his own area without grave risk. The dogmatic theologian who enters any other field must do so with many disclaimers as to his competence.

There is, however, a more profound reason—more profound because it says something about the nature and calling of theology itself. The discipline of theological thinking and the discipline of the life of prayer have become so seriously separated from each other because it is often thought that what one is doing in theology is quite different from what one is doing at prayer. Theology, on the one hand, is seen as conceptual and abstract; it attempts to develop a scientific methodology. In the vast majority of cases within the Christian theological tradition, theologians have intended to be rational and to make use of principles derived from philosophy or some related discipline. Prayer, on the other hand, is usually thought of as highly personal and affective. While prayer does not usually claim to be antirational, it would seem to be at least unrational, uninterested in philosophical concepts or scientific and logical methodology. Indeed, the act of theological thinking and the act of praying do require different disciplines of the mind, for they are not the same thing. Yet we ought to know that the person who writes and teaches theology is also a person who prays; and the person who prays is also one who has to some degree thought about and reflected upon the mystery of God. What a person thinks about God must come from some kind of knowledge of God derived from prayer, and the God to whom one prays must to some degree be the God about whom Christians have thought and spoken. The God of theology and the God to whom we pray are the same God. When these cease to be the same God, both the theologian and the person of prayer are in difficulty.

Each of us, however, must approach another discipline from his place within his own discipline. What I hope to do here is approach the life and the discipline of prayer from my perspective as one who is concerned with the intellectual discipline of theology. That will mean several things. It will mean, primarily, that I shall be concerned to see how the life of prayer is grounded in what we believe about God and ourselves, as that belief has been stated and examined in the long theological tradition of the Christian church. It means that I shall be somewhat less concerned about the methods of prayer and somewhat more concerned about the foundation and direction of the life of prayer. If a theologian has anything to say about the discipline of prayer, it will be by drawing attention to the close, intimate, and essential connection between the life of prayer and that life of thought which results in theology. We can all go desperately wrong in our prayers if they do not rest upon and grow out of theological reflection about God and ourselves, just as we can go desperately wrong when our intellectual formulations about God and ourselves are not grounded in the life of prayer. We must try to see something of the necessary connection between the two, for the God to whom we pray is the God whom we confess in the creeds of the church and about whom we read in Holy Scripture. As we become able to see more and more the connection between praying and thinking, we can at least hope that through the articulation of our belief in him and through our prayers to him, he is more and more making himself known to us, indeed, is educating us into himself.

In this book I have quite intentionally refrained from discussing one aspect of prayer which, for many people today, has become very important, namely, the gift of prayer in tongues. My reason for not discussing that form of prayer is that my knowledge of it is secondhand, derived from conversation and from having read some of the literature about it. Since this is a quite personal book, I did not feel it appropriate to discuss an area in which I should have had to rely upon the writing and experience of others. From what I have learned about that particular gift, however, I am convinced that it should not be seen, as it sometimes is, as a form of prayer which is irrational or even antirational, nor as one which stands in opposition to the ascetical and theological tradition which I have developed here. Indeed, I think it would, at the least, parallel what I have said and might well add a whole new dimension to our understanding of the relationship between praying and thinking. The gift of tongues may well be one of those forms of prayer through which we can even now catch a glimpse of that silence before the mystery of God to which all of us are called. However, the investigation of that possibility must be left to another time and, perhaps, to other people.

During the period when I was preparing this book, I preached a series of sermons in the chapel of the seminary where I teach. In those sermons I attempted to use the ideas with which I was working as the subject and theme for meditation. The sermons were given during Lent, concluding in Holy Week, and they focused on the Gospel account of the temptation of Jesus and how he was, through the temptations presented to him, educated into his vocation and into the ultimate mystery of his relationship with the God whom he called Father. Since Jesus is the paradigm and exemplar for all Christians, how he came to understand his vocation and the mystery of his being is of fundamental importance for us who are called to live in him, and through him to be transformed. Thus the meditations on the temptations of Jesus speak of our education and transformation from the perspective of Jesus himself, and they can provide, I believe, another way of viewing and understanding what it is to say that we are called to union with God. I hope that readers will find those meditations, included in this book, helpful in conjunction with the text itself.

The idea for this book began when I was asked to give a series of informal talks to the Sisters of the Holy Nativity in Fond du Lac, Wisconsin, and I want to thank the Sisters and the Reverend Mother Boniface for that opportunity and for their perceptive comments. The Reverend A. M. Allchin, Canon of Canterbury Cathedral, read the entire manuscript and greatly encouraged and helped me in its development. I should also like to thank my students and colleagues at Nashotah House who have helped me with it in many ways, not least by providing me with a community of prayer in which to think.

James E. Griffiss

Part One

THE SILENCE
OF THE WORD

1

Praying and Thinking

God is a great mystery. That profound theological concept is the one from which all theology must begin and where, finally, it must end. What the Christian tradition has maintained is that such a mystery can be approached by us only through images and symbols, through the things of our experience and through the language with which we try to speak of that which cannot be contained or exhausted by our language. All of us who believe in God have images, symbols, and concepts through which we try to express to ourselves and to others the nature of that mystery in whom we believe and to whom we pray. One of the most essential tasks of the theologian and of the person of prayer is to examine, each in his or her own way, the images we have about that ultimate and final mystery we call God. When a theologian or a person of prayer approaches the various images and concepts that people have of God, his or her concern is not to abolish and destroy them in the belief that better ones can be substituted. Rather, the concern is to show how every image, symbol, and concept we apply to God is always limited and tentative because it is drawn from the limited perception we have of the world around us. The danger for anyone who believes and who seeks to express that belief in any form of language is to take those limited and tentative images and concepts and to make them absolute and final. That is the reason theologians and the great spiritual directors are so often thought to be making life difficult for others; it is their task to show that no one conception and no one image we have of God can ever exhaust that mystery of luminous darkness.

And yet, of course, what all of us want to do is find some one pattern, some one set of images, by means of which we can define and fix once and for all—for ourselves and for others—the nature of God. Despite the naturalness of that desire, and to some degree its inevitability, it is something with which we must be very careful and against which the theological and ascetical disciplines must struggle. The problem is that this desire represents the human tendency toward idolatry. That tendency can be seen very clearly in the Old Testament, where the people of Israel repeatedly attempted to contain the free and transcendent God within categories which they could understand and which, therefore, would give them the impression that they could manipulate and control him. Against this tendency the prophets always brought the word of judgment. God's way cannot be put into a pattern of human liking because he is Creator and Lord. Jesus himself also consistently refused to allow his contemporaries to fit him into a known and accepted pattern or to define precisely his relationship to the One he called Father. Jesus broke through every category by which Judaism attempted to understand him. No human category can adequately explain God's way in history or the bringing in of his kingdom. For Christians today, of course, the same tendency persists in so much of our inability to recognize that God far transcends what our religious tradition has tried to make of him. That is our form of idolatry. And idolatry, whether it be the idol of an image or the idol of a concept, always has the same result. The idolater turns from the one true God to other gods with which it is easier to deal. A god we can control in some manner does not require of us the discipline of education into him.

That is the heart of the problem for all of us, both in our life of prayer and in our life of theological reflection. What we want, and what in various ways we create for ourselves, is a god whom we can control either through our theological concepts or through our prayers. The pilgrimage and education of the person of faith, however, is to attend to the true God and not to the idols we would make. How we attend to him and how we are educated into him is the subject of theology and the practice of prayer. What we are required to discover is that in spite of ourselves we are always called further and further into the mystery of God and to the realization that there is always in him more for us to know and love.

There is a simple way of illustrating what it is to speak of our being educated into God. It is a simple and illuminating illustration drawn from an experience that is familiar to all of us. Consider how it is that we come to know and love others. We meet another person, casually and briefly, to whom for one reason or another we are drawn. It may be physical attraction; it may be what we call wit or charm; it may be great personal strength and depth. For whatever reason, we attempt to establish some kind of continuing contact with that person. We engage in conversation, and through talking to one another we come to a much greater understanding and appreciation of that person than we originally had. We move, indeed, from seeing him or her simply as a rather charming and attractive object to a condition which (if we are fortunate) we can only describe as personal communion—that kind of relationship between persons which we describe variously as love or friendship. All that is common enough, but when we reflect upon what has happened we begin to realize something of great importance. We begin to realize that a person whom we love, whom we are in the process of coming to know and understand, is never just an object which can be precisely and definitively defined and categorized. Everyone has had the experience of having preconceptions shattered by something new in the personality of another. We can suddenly discover in the personality of another a whole new depth we had not seen before. As Christians, we can say about this experience that we have been surprised by grace. Coming to know and love another person can be for us an example of what we mean when we say that God is a mystery into whom we are being educated. The experience we have can show us something of what that theological statement means. A person is one who is constantly revealing more and more of himself as we come into communion with him; he is one who is always showing us that there is more than we can ever fully grasp and understand.

In various forms the Christian tradition has tried to say that we are being educated into the mystery of God in a manner similar to what happens between persons. God is one who, as we pray to him and think about him, constantly reveals more and more of himself to us and who thereby transforms those idols we would erect in his place. Theologians, poets, spiritual directors, and ordinary Christians have witnessed to the possibility of that kind of personal communion with the God in whom we grow, by whom we are transformed, and about whom we discover, by grace, that he is a mystery who can never be exhausted by anything we may say about him. Thomas Aquinas, for example, began his discussion of the doctrine of God by saying that we can never know what God is, for the mystery of his nature surpasses the limitations of our intellect. All we can say about God is what he is not, for we can speak of that mystery only in an oblique way. Gregory of Nyssa, speaking of Moses when he entered the Cloud of the Presence of Mount Sinai, says that God is a luminous darkness, using an image which is repeated over and over again in Christian literature. Dante speaks of the vision of God as a vision of light, and the psalmist speaks of God as clothed in light. Each of these images, and there are many more, attempt to point us in the direction of God as the mystery that cannot be grasped but in whose light we live.

To think of God and to visualize him in this way points to the relationship, indeed, the unity, of the life of prayer and theology. Thinking and praying are different, but their root is the same, and it is that common root which we must discover.

What is common to ascetical theology, which traditionally has dealt with the discipline of prayer, and systematic or dogmatic theology, which has traditionally dealt with the conceptual formulation of doctrine, is theology itself. Both are theology, even though we sometimes use that word as though it referred only to the conceptual formulation of Christian belief. What is theology for the Christian—theology, not in some narrow or academic sense, but in its widest breadth? The word itself, of course, is formed of two Greek words: *theos,* God, and *logos,* which is usually translated into English to mean "the study of something." That is, however, a rather weak and insipid definition of one of the richest words in that very rich language, classical

Greek. And even more, here we are concerned with the *logos* of *theos*. What would it mean to make a study of God? Even to put the question in that form points to something of a human presumption.   .

In the richness of the Greek word *logos,* on the other hand, there is one fundamental meaning which can help us to see the meaning of theology more clearly. *Logos* means primarily a word —the word we speak and also the mental word or concept we are attempting to communicate through our spoken word. *Logos* involves communication, how we seek to communicate with one another through the spoken language. Language is one of the ways in which we seek to relate ourselves to others, to express ourselves, to move out from our own internal world to the world of other people. But in the Christian tradition the word *logos* has not only been used to refer to the words we use to communicate with one another. From the time of the writing of the Fourth Gospel it has been applied to Jesus Christ himself. In the Gospel of John the term *logos* was used to express something about what the early Christian community believed about Jesus of Nazareth. He was called the *Logos* of God: God's Word, God's act of self-communication, God's self-expression to us. What the identification of God's *logos* with Jesus of Nazareth accomplished in the history of Christian doctrine is profoundly important. Among other things, it enabled the early Christian community to reflect upon the relationship between its own faith in a crucified and risen Jew from Palestine and the wider course of divine activity in the creation. As early as the second century, Justin Martyr was able to say that the *logos* of God, made known in Jesus Christ, is that same *logos* by which pagans live in their own search for meaning and value. It also enabled the Jewish-Christian community to find a theological basis for the communication of the gospel to those who did not share the history and the theological categories of Judaism. Without such a development it is difficult to imagine how the gospel could have been preached outside the Judaism of the Old Covenant. The identification of Jesus of Nazareth with the *logos* established a point of contact with the Greek and Roman world of philosophy and culture. Finally, the use of the word enabled the early church to see something more of the nature of theology itself (as can be seen in the theological definitions of the early councils). This connection is especially important here.

To understand theology as the *logos* of *theos* suggests that we must begin to see that the theological discipline, whether it be that of the life of prayer or whether it be that of doctrinal conceptualization, involves more than what we say about God in our theology and more than what we say to him in our prayers. If all that were involved in theology was our own words, it would not get us very far, because we should in the end be talking only to ourselves. One thing we learn from prayer (and it is something the theologian ought also to learn from his own discipline) is that we must learn to listen to what God says to us. Theology, in its broadest sense, involves not only what we say to God and about him but also what he says to us and about us in his word, in his act of self-communication. Our words to and about God are important and essential because they form a part of the process by means of which we make clear to ourselves, to others, and finally to God what we believe about him and what we need to bring before him out of our own lives. They are our process of communicating; and, as we all know from our attempts at communication, it is as we speak and try to express ourselves that we begin to understand what we believe about important things. That the early church soon saw the identity of Jesus with the word of God, however, points to something more in this process of communication. It means that in some manner or form God also communicates with us. He expresses himself in our history, not simply in a vague and general way, but concretely in a person. The long history of the church's reflection upon the doctrine of Christ has been our attempt to deal with the experience which for all of us is central to our faith, namely, that God in Christ has made himself known to us in his Logos, that is, in his eternal Son. This is the confession of faith which the conciliar fathers struggled to express as the doctrine of the Trinity. That God speaks his word to us has many fundamental consequences for our lives of prayer and our thinking, and it is a matter to which we must return in a later chapter.

Implicit in what I have been saying about *logos* is the prob-

lem of the language which we use to and about God in our praying and thinking. The nature of language is one of the central
problems in any theology. God, we believe, no matter how we
may finally want to explain that name in conceptual language,
transcends our ordinary experience. The language we use to
describe tables and chairs is certainly not completely appropriate
to describe the ultimate source of all reality. The closest analogy
we have, even though it also is by no means completely ade-
quate, is the language we use to describe our relations with
other human beings. In prayer and in theology, we usually
speak to God and about God as though he were another person,
and yet we know that our speaking to him and about him is not
just the same as speaking to or about a friend. He is more than
that. It is, therefore, essential for us to be aware of the difficulties involved as soon as we begin to think about what it means to
speak words to God and about him, and for him to speak his
word to us. When we begin to think about that problem we can,
I believe, see two important things. First, we can see that our
words to and about God always point to his word to and about
us. Second, we can see that any language which attempts to
communicate something about God both shares in and does not
share in the structure of the language we use every day in order
to talk about the world of our ordinary experience. That God
speaks to us and about us is what we mean when we talk about
revelation. Revelation is the word of judgment which is spoken
to us in Jesus Christ; it shows us not only what we are but also
what we are called to become. It is the Word of God which must
illuminate all our words about God, and it is that Word which
finally makes our words possible. Our words form part of the
process by which his word speaks to us. That we can speak to and
about God points us also to a way of understanding who we are
as creatures who always stand with our feet firmly on the ground
from which we were made (for we are always creatures), but who
are yet called beyond ourselves to some form of communication
and communion with him who creates us and who makes our
words possible.

This is the theological point of view that forms the basis for all
that follows. What we must consider is that which unites God's

word to us and to our words to and about him—that common root to which I referred earlier. What unites them is the common source of our words of prayer and our words of theology. It is an activity that characterizes us as creatures who are called to God and that roots our words in the divine Word. That activity is what I shall call the silence of thanksgiving.

We usually think of silence not as an activity but as a state of not talking. But to be silent is an act, and not just a passive state, because to be silent means to attend, to pay attention to another. To be silent means to listen and to hear; it means to reflect upon what is and what is said. It is, in other words, an intense form of communication through which we can enter into communion with another person and with God. We are silent with a person we love, not because there is nothing to be said but because everything is being said and has been said. It is an activity in which, as we attend, hear, and reflect upon it, the word which God speaks to us becomes that internal word out of which all our other words must come. Paul speaks in a similar vein when he tells us to let this mind be in us which is also in Christ Jesus: God's word forms our words.

It is, then, with the theological dimension of silence that I shall be concerned. Silence is an activity of our spiritual lives and is a theological principle which will enable us to see more clearly who we are in relation to God and who we are called to become. There is considerable justification in the theological and ascetical tradition for such an approach, and it is, of course, central to the mystical tradition. But there are two examples that can be especially helpful. The first is from the Catholic theologian Thomas Aquinas, the second from the Danish Christian Søren Kierkegaard.

In his beautiful and profound little book *The Silence of St. Thomas,* Josef Pieper explores the theological significance of silence in Aquinas's approach to God and tells the familiar story that so well illustrates what silence came to mean to Aquinas himself. At the end of his life he found that he could no longer speak or write about God, and he said that the reason for this was that compared to what had been shown him of that mystery, all he had written was like straw. Pieper says:

The last word of St. Thomas is no communication but silence. And it is not death which takes the pen out of his hand. His tongue is stilled by the superabundance of life in the mystery of God. He is silent not because he has nothing further to say; he is silent because he has been allowed a glimpse into the inexpressible depths of that mystery which is not reached by any human thought or speech.[1]

All his words about God and to God return finally into that silence from which they came.

Many differences separate the world of Thomas Aquinas from that of Kierkegaard, but both were confronted by the same reality of God. Kierkegaard, speaking of the man of prayer, says that which Aquinas and any other person of prayer would also say:

In proportion as he became more and more earnest in prayer he had less and less to say, and in the end he became quite silent. He became silent—indeed what is if possible still more expressly the opposite of speaking, he became a hearer. He had supposed that to pray is to speak; he learnt that to pray is not merely to be silent, but it is to be silent, and to remain silent, to wait, until the man who prays hears God.[2]

2

To Be a Person

We have seen something of the two areas in which the common root of our words and God's word to us can be found. God speaks his word to us primarily in his revelation of himself in Jesus Christ. To that Word, and to a consideration of its significance for every word we speak, we shall return later. Now we shall be concerned with the words we speak, for those of us who are Christians believe that we have spoken to God and that we can, in one way or another, speak about him. That speaking is the beginning of our spiritual life. What does it say about us, both about what we are now and about what we are called to become, that we are not only able to speak to and about God but that we desire to do so?

There are many different ways in which we can attempt to understand what a human being is. A sociologist, for example, might well try to understand human nature through an analysis of how men and women live and conduct themselves in a social situation. Psychologists might concern themselves with behavior patterns, biologists with our similarities to other living beings. A philosopher might be concerned with human culture and language, with the fact that human beings ask questions of themselves and of their world. All these are valid and necessary approaches to understanding the human animal, and the theologian must use all of them, for they show from many different perspectives what it is to be human. With such complex beings, the more ways in which we can see ourselves and how we function, the better we shall understand ourselves. Christians, however, will want to add their own perspective, for we believe that in order to have an accurate description of human beings they must always be seen in terms of their relationship with that reality we call God. Indeed, we should want to say that only as they are understood in terms of that relationship with God can their humanity be understood. For Christians, that is the most fundamental truth about our common humanity.

In saying that, however, we must be very careful, for there are several dangerous traps into which it is possible to fall, and into which Christians indeed have fallen from time to time. Just as a limited conception of God can have disastrous effects for our spirituality, so too can a limited conception of human beings in their relationship to God. In the first and most obvious way, we do not want to say, when we speak of ourselves in relation to God, that human beings therefore ought to live in another, vaguely spiritual world, unrelated to the problems and concerns of time and space. Because it is an incarnational faith, Christianity can never seek to remove people from the world into which the word of God has come. It would be very wrong as well as dangerous for us to say that our relationship to God requires of us an escape from this world. Human beings are political, social, economic, biological, and psychological beings; and it must be precisely in all those relationships that we seek to understand our relationship to God. Human beings, as they are related to God, are not just religious.

The second danger follows from the first. It has been one of the most persistent problems in the approach taken to spirituality by many in our time. It is the illusion or belief that our relationship to God is exclusively our own concern, an individual and private matter. If we lose sight of God's act in the world, that is, if we lose sight of the Incarnation, then it becomes easy for us to believe that the only thing with which we need be concerned is our own individual piety. Because of this kind of individualistic piety it is possible to fail to see that there is a connection between the state of one's soul and what one does every day in the world. When that happens, prayer can easily become a form of escape from our obligations to others and to the world around us rather than one of the most appropriate responses we can make to the world and its needs.

Both these dangers afflict the church today. As many men

and women turned in despair from the failure of social activism in the last decade, they have often retreated into a nonincarnational separation of the church from the human situation, and they have tended to see the church and personal piety as concerned only with unworldly matters. That is not only a denial of Christian responsibility but also (and for that reason) a false understanding of spirituality. That is not what the New Testament means when it speaks of men and women as spiritual beings. What spirituality means, both in the New Testament and in the Christian tradition, therefore, is something we must examine more carefully.

To speak at all about human spirituality, however, raises a problem immediately. Someone might well ask if the idea of God and the possibility of prayer to him and of reasonable words about him are simply a delusion. Is it necessary to establish the reasonable possibility of theism before we begin to discuss such a thing as human spirituality? I believe not, not only for the immediate purpose of discussing human spirituality but for any theological discussion within the community of faith. It certainly is necessary to do a great deal of clarifying about our concept of God and our words to him, and we must do that not only for ourselves but also for the sake of those to whom we would speak of God. But the experience that human beings have within the church (which can be found in many other religious traditions as well) is the foundation from which we can begin. That experience varies with individuals, and for some it is not as articulate or well-formed as for others. For those, however, who have been involved to some degree in the life of prayer or in the life of theological reflection, and who have been concerned to live out the consequences of the particular vocation to which they have been called, there is no more need to demonstrate God's reality or to justify their relationship to him than there is a necessity to demonstrate or justify the reality of another person whom we have known and loved. Indeed, most theologians today, in the light of the many philosophical and theological problems involved in this area, would say that the reality, the ''existence'' of God cannot be rationally demonstrated to those who do not have to some degree an awareness of a relationship with him. In some older forms of theology such demonstrations were attempted, and for certain theological systems they perform the valuable function of showing the relationship between the life of reason and the life of faith. Generally, however, such attempts have not been convincing to those who have not already experienced something of God's reality, even though they may help those who do believe to understand more deeply the reality of God in their lives. But here we are speaking from within the community of faith, that is to say, from within that body of people who believe that the structure of their lives and of the world around them is one which demands belief not only in some kind of transcendent reality but in One who has made himself known to us in many different ways, primarily in the center of our faith, Jesus Christ. Because we believe as we do, we believe that we are able to understand and interpret the world of our experience in a way which is not irrational or delusory. Although we must recognize that the meaning of life which Christians find in God is not so understood by many others, nonetheless we believe that there is no other way which makes any sense for us in terms of our experience of ourselves and our world. This is to speak from faith, not in justification of faith. The justification of faith must be found, if it is to be found at all, elsewhere in our lives. When at a later time we consider the context of belief within which God's word and will confronts us this is a matter which will be of great importance.

To speak from faith, rather than in justification of faith, can give us a starting point for our exploration of ourselves as we stand in relation to God, that is, to speak of human beings as spiritual. While we are not seeking to justify our faith in a transcendent reality, we can and ought to ask ourselves what there is about us that makes it possible for us to have such a faith. Why is it that we are not content to explain ourselves and the world in which we live solely in their own terms? Why is it that in order to understand ourselves and our world we seek for an explanation in something which transcends us and our world? This kind of question has often fascinated theologians and some philosophers, and it is a question which can be found in the biblical narrative as well. That we do it is a fact, but why do we do it? What does it say about us as human beings that we are able and desirous through our language, concepts, images, and myths to transcend our immediate experience and to find the meaning of ourselves and our world in a transcendent reality?

In the history of Western philosophy and theology one concept has been used to explain that capacity and desire in human beings to understand themselves in relation to the transcendent. It is the concept of the soul. Like all important words, its history has been varied; it has been a more or a less important concept at different periods. Generally speaking, however, the concept of the soul has been used to point to two dimensions in human self-understanding: our rationality and our spirituality. The concept of the soul has suggested that there is always more to be said about a human being than that which can be contained within a particular history between birth and death. Despite the misuse to which it has often been put in the Christian tradition, the concept of the soul is important because it has been used to point to an eternal dimension in human beings and to provide a way in which we could talk about our rationality and spirituality. To understand the rational dimension of human beings as rooted in the soul means that rationality itself cannot be limited to our problem-solving ability but that in some way it points to a ground in a transcendent reality. Similarly, to speak of our spirituality in terms of the soul means that human beings, in their very nature, in their createdness, are in some way or other related fundamentally to God. Both these considerations can give us some insight into our human capacity to speak to and about God and to hear God's word when it is spoken to us. To understand our rationality and spirituality as directing us toward God is a theme deeply rooted in the biblical tradition, and that is the point from which we can begin.

The biblical tradition begins with the story of the creation of the world and of man and woman. That story provides the basic structure through which the relation of human beings to God in their rationality and spirituality must be understood. It is, of course, important to recognize that the story of creation in the Book of Genesis was an editing of much more ancient material which had formed a part of Israel's oral tradition. It was largely gathered by a group Old Testament scholars call the Priestly editors. The intention of these editors was to show that the foundation and significance of Israel's history could be found only in the covenant they had with God—that intimate relationship which was unique to Israel among the nations of the Middle East. The Priestly editors attempt to show that from its very origins Israel had existed in a special relationship with God and that their God was not a local or tribal deity but in fact the Lord of the whole creation. The story of creation has its foundation in the experience Israel had had throughout its history, namely, that God had called this people into the life of the covenant. Thus, from the very beginning of their narrative the editors wished to show that the God whom they had known as the Lord of their own history was the Lord of all history. It is in this context that the story of the creation of man and woman must be understood.

What is also fundamental to the Genesis story is that the writers saw the world as having its origin and its unity and coherence in a completely personal will and not in an abstract principle or in the struggle among various gods or powers, as in the case of so many mythologies. God the Lord creates the world out of his own freedom. For this reason the narrative does not make any reference to the origin of God himself. God is there in the beginning, and whatever happens is a result of his free and sovereign will. The creation is not a natural emanation from God but a creative act. This conception had a radical effect upon how the Jews understood the relation of the world to God. The word they used for *"create"* was *bara*, a word which points to the calling of the world into existence rather than the fashioning or forming of it from something else. From the very beginning, God calls the creation, and he continues to call it. For the biblical tradition the creative act of God is a continuous activity. Creation is not something which took place in the distant past and which can therefore now be ignored. To speak of creation is to speak of how God always relates himself to the world; it is his continuous saving activity which Israel continues to discover in its life in the covenant.

Only on such terms is it possible to understand the story of the creation of man and woman. In the Genesis narrative, Adam and Eve stand at the height of the created order because they are patterned after God himself. They are a part of the creation, but because they are created in the image of God, they cannot be understood exclusively in terms of the created order. The explanation of human beings lies not in the created order but outside it, in God. As Old Testament scholar Gerhard von Rad suggests, it is more correct to say that Israel's conception of man is theomorphic than that its conception of God is anthropomorphic. As Yahweh is the Lord of the whole creation, human beings have the status of lord in the world. Thus, in their very createdness they have a particular ordering toward God. Their feet always stand on the earth from which they were created, but they are called to God, and they can understand themselves only in terms of that calling which is a part of their createdness. The full significance of this way of understanding human beings is found in the story of the Fall. The temptation to which human beings in Adam and Eve succumb is precisely in that dimension of themselves which is most central to their nature as those who are called to God in their very existence as creatures. Human beings can be tempted because they are created in the image of God; if that were not true of them, they could not be tempted. So, what the serpent says to Adam and Eve touches them at their most vulnerable and vital point (as temptation always touches us), because the temptation is to become "like God" rather than to fulfill the calling to live in God's image. Human beings are tempted to expand themselves, so to speak, on their godward side and to reject their existence as creatures who are called to obedience. We who are created in the *imago dei* seek to become *sicut deus* (like God). Dietrich Bonhoeffer well says of this temptation and of its redemption in Christ: "*Imago dei, sicut deus, agnus dei*—the One who was sacrificed for man *sicut deus*, killing man's false divinity in true divinity, the God-Man who restores the image of God."[1] The calling of human beings, the structure through which we as *imago dei* must always be understood, is that God calls us to obedience to our vocation. The long history of Israel was the history of the struggle of this people to be obedient to God's will for them. The prophets saw the fulfillment of that obedience first in Israel's faithfulness to Yahwah and their rejection of other gods, and second in the obligation, which flowed from that, to do justice and mercy to God's people. The prophet Isaiah later interpreted that double calling through his image of an Israel called upon to suffer and so to be a light to other nations. The great tradition of the Law was also seen as God's word to Israel about the structure and obligations of life in every area. The Old Testament has a common theme: Human beings are called to live in relationship with God, and that calling involves them in a life of obedience to the One who is Lord. Anything else is sin, a denial of our createdness and of our relation to God.

In the theology of Paul, as he struggled to understand the meaning of Jesus Christ through his own heritage as a Jew, this way of understanding human existence and of understanding Jesus himself became a fundamental theme. When Paul speaks of human beings as spiritual, and when he contrasts the flesh with the spirit, he is always referring to that dimension of those who, as creatures, are called into relationship with their creator in radical obedience.[2] In Jesus we can see the fulfillment of that vocation—which belonged first to Israel but which is now extended to all people. Jesus in his obedience even to the cross fulfills Adam's disobedience. His life of obedience is proclaimed and established for all in his resurrection from the dead. In the cross he shows us what we truly are: those who are called to a life of obedience in relation to God. So Paul can say that in Christ we are called to the same calling—to be children of God and, with Jesus, heirs to eternal life. Only in the obedience of the cross and in the resurrection to life can the structure of our lives as spiritual creatures be understood.

It is possible to trace in the theological tradition of Christianity how that basic theme has been expanded and developed and how, at times, it has been obscured and forgotten. This basic theme can be seen clearly, for example, in the Greek fathers as they struggled to state the doctrine of the Incarnation as the personal unity of humanity with God in Christ. It can be seen also in Augustine, who could write that we are restless until we find our rest in God. It can also be seen in Thomas Aquinas, as he attempted to define the relationship between the order of nature and the action of God in grace. And it can be seen in our day in the attempt of many modern theologians to use new images and concepts in order to recover this fundamental insight into the nature and calling of all human beings.

What that long theological tradition has said in many different ways is that in terms of their historical existence as creatures, that is, as those who are dependent upon God for their existence, human beings are called to unity with God. They have a divine destiny which perfects and fulfills their existence as creatures rather than destroying it. In our day, the term *person* most fully expresses for us how we can understand ourselves in relation to others and to God. It is a term with a long history. Much of the richness it now has is derived from its theological development in the controversies over the doctrine of the Incarnation and the doctrine of the Trinity. The meaning of the term has been sharpened and defined more precisely by developments in philosophy and psychology during the past one hundred years. At the present time, the word *person* is generally used to refer to those people who can act out of themselves, who are centered, who have a sense of self-identity and personal history. Persons are those who can act consciously and responsibly and who, when they do not, can reflect back upon themselves and judge what they have failed to do. In this sense, persons have personality; they are those who shine out and about whom we can say that they are in process toward something more than they now are or have been in the past.

In the Christian theological tradition, there are two dogmatic formulations which illuminate the meaning of the word *person* and which have also helped to shape the meaning it now has. Both the formulations are central to the Christian faith, because they state what we believe about God and his act toward us in Christ. In each the church was struggling to say something about the meaning of personhood within the context of particular theological debates, but what was said then can and ought to inform what we, in another situation, want to say today. What the church has witnessed to about Jesus Christ and what it has tried to define in various ways is that in the incarnation of the eternal Logos our humanity is personally united to God in the humanity of Jesus himself. In all the struggles of doctrinal history, the mystery of two natures, divine and human, in personal unity has remained central to our confession of faith in Jesus Christ. Why it has remained central, despite necessary developments in language and imagery, can be seen in a statement attributed to Athanasius: "The Son of God became son of man so that the sons of men, that is, of Adam, might become sons of God . . . partakers of the life of God. . . . Thus he is Son of God by nature, and we by grace."[3] In the person of Jesus Christ, human beings are called to be partakers of the divine nature. Whatever we may want to say about ourselves as persons must take its start from Jesus Christ himself, for to be a person is to be one who in his eternal destiny is called to be united to God. That is the foundation for our understanding of ourselves as spiritual creatures.

The second dogmatic formulation concerns the doctrine of God as Trinity. In that doctrine, again within a particular historical and linguistic context, the church struggled to articulate its belief that the highest form of unity, the unity of God himself, is the unity of persons. The personal unity of the Godhead must always be for us the structure through which we understand our own existence as spiritual creatures who are called to a participation in the life of the Trinity. What we mean by *person*, as we use the word in ordinary language, can illuminate for us what we believe about God, but at the same time what we mean by the word is grounded in what God has made known of himself in the work of the Son and Holy Spirit.

On the basis of these central dogmatic formulations about the Person of Christ and the personal unity of God as Trinity, we can see something of great importance about our nature and calling as spiritual beings. They point to those two qualities which most deeply and profoundly express what it is to be a person, namely, that a person is one who is free and who in his freedom is able to love others.

Persons are free in the sense that they are centered beings who have some degree of responsibility for their actions. We are able to say that persons have acted irresponsibly precisely because we can recognize them as those who must take responsibility for what they do and what they are. In the traditional terminology of ethics, this is what was meant by conscience: a person can know what is right and can choose the good; a person is a moral agent. If we consider, for example, how we deal with the past and the present in our own lives, we can see that more clearly. An animal is limited by its past and present experience. It is not able to transcend the present or the past and come to an understanding of their meaning and significance for its whole life. We, however, are able to reflect upon the past and the present, to make judgments about them, to see where we went wrong and where we were right in what we did, and so to plan a course of future action. We are able, in other words, to think about ourselves and our world as something which is not finally and totally determined by what has happened to us in the past or is happening to us in the present. Because that kind of reflection is something we do much of the time, it is easy for us to overlook its significance. Human beings can think; that is one of the most important things that can be said about us. We can reflect upon ourselves, and we want to do so—both are equally important. A free and rational being is one who is able to think, judge, plan, and look toward the future with expectation and hope. He is able to transcend the immediacy of the present moment. To be able to do that and to want to do it is to be a person. It is, in fact, another way of saying that human beings have been created in the image of God and that they are called to live obediently in that image. Obedience implies the freedom both to will and to think, just as disobedience implies a slavery to sin and death. Free and spiritual persons, as Paul says, are "in Christ," that is, they are able to live toward God rather than be dominated and destroyed by the past of their failures and sins. That they know themselves called to do that is to be forgiven and set free.

The second characteristic of persons is that they are free to love others. Human spirituality is expressed fundamentally in the fact that we desire to and are able to enter into significant relationships, that we find our meaning as persons not in ourselves but in others—in our neighbor and in God. The biblical tradition speaks of this dimension of human spirituality through the figures of Adam and Christ. The sin of Adam was concupiscence and pride. Through disobedience to his vocation to live in the image of God, Adam turned into himself and in his pride saw himself, rather than the God who had created him, as lord of all things. So it is also with us. The distortion of love, as we all know, is our attempt to live for ourselves and to see all others, including God, as instruments or means to serve us rather than as those whom we are to serve. In the life of obedient service which is shown to us in Jesus, we are enabled to see that we are called to serve others, to find our meaning and purpose in life as we live not for ourselves but for others. Seen from the point of view of our calling to love another, to be persons means to find fulfillment in two places. First, to be persons is to find fulfillment in the human community formed by the Holy Spirit in the death and resurrection of Christ. Second, to be persons is to find fulfillment in God who is a trinity of persons. Christians are those who believe that in the church they are called to become persons who are free to love others in order that every man and woman can be personally united to God.

To speak of our humanity as spiritual, then, is to speak of ourselves as those who are called to personal unity with God and with all people. Through the transformation of our lives by the Holy Spirit, we are called to become what the reconciling work of God in Christ has created in us. This is the force behind Paul's injunction to the Corinthians: ''Do you not know that your body is a shrine of the indwelling Holy Spirit, and the Spirit is God's gift to you? You do not belong to yourselves; you were bought at a price'' (1 Cor. 6:19). In a similar way Cyprian could say that the church is the sacrament of unity because it is now the cause, expression, and symbol of that final unity of all people with God and among themselves through their sharing in the unity of the Father, Son, and Holy Spirit.[4] The spiritual person is one for whom the meaning of the past and the present is always found in a call to a future glory. Through that hope we understand ourselves now, for it is the structure and purpose of our present life in the community of faith. But not yet, for God always calls us beyond even our present understanding into a greater mystery, that is, into himself. It is about that mystery that we speak, and it is to that mystery that we pray.

3

To Speak about God

In the last chapter we began to see how the biblical doctrine of man can give us an insight into what it means to speak of human spirituality. If we are faithful to the biblical picture, then we shall want to say that the spirituality of human beings does not mean something special and unique to one group of people as opposed to another; nor does it mean something about them which removes them from time and space and the course of human history. What we do mean is that human beings are rooted in the earth as creatures, and precisely as that they are called to God as their destiny. It is the historical, spatial, temporal man and woman, with all the limitations and difficulties implied in such an existence, who are spiritual. To be human is to be spirit in the world. At the same time, however, we are called to God; we are called beyond ourselves to another, and we are at rest not solely in ourselves. We cannot be fully and completely understood unless that transcendent dimension of our being is considered also. What we now need to explore is how that transcendent dimension can be seen more clearly in terms of the particular vocation we have as spiritual persons.

The dimension of transcendence can be seen in many different ways. As we shall see later, it can be glimpsed through the way in which we understand ourselves as free and loving persons. Here I want to speak of transcendence in another way, namely, in terms of the fact that we have language. What does it say about us that we are able to speak and to communicate through words? Paul Tillich has written:

> As long as he is human, that is, as long as he has not "fallen" from humanity (e.g. in intoxication or insanity), man never is

37

bound completely to an environment. He always transcends it by grasping and shaping it according to universal norms and ideas. Even in the most limited environment man possesses the universe; he has a world. Language, as the power of universals, is the basic expression of man's transcending of his environment, of having a world. The ego-self is that self which can speak and which by speaking trespasses the boundaries of any given situation.[1]

Tillich's point is true even of the language we use about perfectly ordinary things in our everyday experience. When I am able to say, for example, of some object in front of me, "This is a chair," I have done thereby that which no animal can do. I have, by insight and judgment, identified and named an object, and I have united myself to the long history of human reason and language. I have transcended the immediacy of my environment through the word which I have spoken, and I have joined the human community of those who communicate to one another through the spoken word. Even more than that, however, our words, and the structure of language through which we speak, are our encounter with mystery—both with the mystery of things and the mystery of God.

The word *mystery,* like all important words, has a long and complex history. Most of us think of a mystery as something like a problem. If only we know enough about a certain situation, we can solve the mystery of it. Here, however, I shall be using the word in the sense in which it is used in the New Testament and elsewhere in the theological tradition. A mystery is not something we can solve if only we know enough facts; on the contrary, it is something which can never be exhausted by all the knowledge we may have of it. To know a mystery is always to know that more is there than we can ever penetrate and know completely. In this sense we must say, for example, that another person is a mystery because, try as we might, we can never know completely the reality of another person. Mystery is an essential concept in theology because it shows us that the world and the people in it can never be reduced totally to a technological or functional interpretation. They are always more than what we know about them. We enter into a mystery; indeed, we are called into it. It is in this sense that we can think about words and the structure of language itself as our encounter with mystery.

Out of what do our words and language arise? Consider what happens when we find ourselves in the presence of an unknown object. I look at it and wonder what it is. I may take it in my hand and feel it or turn it over in order to see it better. I may try to taste it or smell it. I want to know what it is, to be able to identify it, to relate it to other things about me, to find out what it is for, to give it a name. This is an experience so common to us that it is easy to overlook how significant it is. A human being, when placed before an object, wonders about it, that is, wants to understand and know something. Out of that wonder arises his attempt to name the thing before him and to place it in the larger context of his experience of a world. We do this for two reasons: first, it enables us to know the object for ourselves, because to name something is to identify what it is; second, it enables us to communicate our knowledge to others. When I say, "This is a chair," I have named an object for myself by locating it within the broader range of my experience of the world, and I have said that the object is this and not something else. By naming an object I know something about it for myself and for anyone to whom I wish to communicate that knowledge. In the Old Testament account of creation, the act of naming something is deeply important. The first thing Adam does is name the objects he sees around him. To wonder and to name are fundamental human acts.

Wonder is our initial reaction to a world of things and arises out of our existence as creatures who are made in the image of God. Human beings are rational. We are able to know, and we desire to know, something about the world in which we find ourselves. "The desire to know . . . is . . . the inquiring and critical spirit of man."[2] But in addition to that, we wonder at things because they are themselves intelligible; they can be known by us. They have, if one may speak this way, a reality which calls us to them. That things are knowable has been spoken of in a variety of ways in the theological and philosophical tradition. It has been called essence, intelligibility, the nature or truth of things. But there is another term, drawn from the theological tradition, which points even more clearly to the intelligibility of the world of things: light. Things are luminous; they shine. Thomas Aquinas, for whom the image of light was of great importance, says, "The measure of the reality of a thing is the measure of its light." And again, "The reality of things is itself their light." Otto Pieper says of this quality of things in the theology of Thomas Aquinas:

> It is the creative fashioning of things by God which *makes it possible* for them to be known by men. What does this signify? It signifies that things can be known by us because God has creatively thought them; as creatively thought by God, things have not only their own nature . . . but as creatively thought by God, things have also a reality "for us." Things have their intelligibility, their inner clarity and lucidity, and the power to reveal themselves because God has creatively thought them. This is why they are essentially intelligible. Their brightness and radiance is infused into things from the creative mind of God, together with their essential being. . . . It is this radiance, and this alone, that makes existing things perceptible to human knowledge. . . . It is this light that makes things perceptible to our eyes. To put it succinctly, things are knowable because they have been created.[3]

For those of us who look at the world from the perspective of belief in God, we can say that things call us to them; they call us beyond ourselves to the One who made them and sustains them in being. To believe that is the consequence of believing that God is Creator; and to say that is to say that our wonder at the mystery of things—tables, chairs, or other people—is a sign of our wonder before the mystery of God. The word we speak when we name a thing is something deeper than would first appear. When I know what something is and name it as such, I have spoken a word of truth, not just engaged in idle chatter. I have, in an initial way, spoken about God who is the truth of all created being. My word is my participation in the intelligibility of God who is the light of all things. The word I speak is an act of communion with the uncreated source of all things, just as it is an act of communion with others to whom I may speak. The word I speak communicates to another person the reality that I have perceived, and another person is able to hear and understand the word of truth that I speak. The word spoken stands between us as the focus through which my reality and the reality of another person are communicated to one another and through which we enter into communion with one another. In the words that we speak, the light, which is our own spirit and intelligibility, can shine forth. The word spoken is an act through which light shines. Paul speaks of this in another way when he says that by the word of preaching faith comes. The word that we speak opens something up; it does not just communicate information. That word makes something visible and brings it to light. For the Christian, what it brings to light is the truth that is in Christ Jesus. The mystery that is shown to us in the preaching of the word is the mystery of God himself, which we meet in Jesus. This mystery is, finally, the same mystery that we meet in tables and chairs and other people, for there is nothing in the order of created things that does not shine with the luminosity of God. That in Jesus that luminosity is particularly clear and apparent to us and that it shines with a special, even unique, brightness is the reason we say that in him the *logos* of God has come among us. But it is also the reason we are able to see the same luminosity in every area of created being. Augustine, quoting the Psalms, referred to Christ as that light by which we see light: Because of Christ, we are able to encounter the mystery of God in all created things.[4] It is to that light that our words about things direct us.

If our words about things open us onto the mystery of God, what does that suggest for the words we speak about God himself? From what do those rather odd words arise, and to what do they lead us? It could be said, and indeed it has been said by some, that any words we might use about God are only a sign of our human presumption to speak about that in the face of which we ought to remain silent. But Christians, and those of other religious traditions as well, have always struggled to say something about that divine nature which we call God, even if only to deny that we can say anything at all. We have believed that our ordinary words can be for us signs or images of God's word spoken to us. Augustine, for example, when speaking of the mystery of the Trinity, concludes that it is not easy to find one term which appropriately defines so great an excellence, but he then goes on to say: "God has accepted the tribute of the human voice and has wished us to praise him in our own language. This is why he is called God, although he is not in reality recognized in the sound of the word, but when we hear the word we ponder his wonderful nature."⁵ To speak about God is not to believe that we have adequately described him but rather to stand in wonder before who he is. Our words about him are always limited to their source in finite experience, and they can only point to, are only partial images of, the God of whom we would speak. But our words do point to him, however unclearly. They are signs, a beginning on the way, so to speak. As signs they are very important, but they are not the end of the journey. The end of the journey can only be silence before the mystery of God. Something of the nature and of the end of that journey from words into silence can be seen in Gregory of Nyssa's meditation on the vision of God which was given to Moses.

Words

> But what now is the meaning of Moses' entry into the darkness and of the vision of God that he enjoyed in it? The present text (Exod. 24:15) would seem to be somewhat contradictory to the divine apparition he has seen before. There he saw God in the light, whereas here he sees him in the darkness. But we should not therefore think that this contradicts the entire sequence of spiritual lessons which we have been considering. For the sacred text is here teaching us that spiritual knowledge first occurs as an illumination in those who experience it. Indeed, all that is opposed to piety is conceived of as darkness; to shun the darkness is to share in the light. But as the soul makes progress, and by a greater and more perfect concentration comes to appreciate what the knowledge of truth is, the more it approaches this vision, and so much the more does it see that the divine nature is invisible. It thus leaves all surface appearances, not only those that can be grasped by the senses but also those which the mind itself seems to see, and it keeps on going deeper until by the operation of the spirit it penetrates the invisible and incomprehensible, and it is there that it sees God. The true vision and the true knowledge of what we seek consists precisely in not seeing, in an awareness that

our goal transcends all knowledge and is everywhere cut off from us by the darkness of incomprehensibility. Thus that profound evangelist, John, who penetrated into this luminous darkness, tells us that *no man hath seen God at any time* (John 1:18), teaching us by this negation that no man—indeed no created intellect—can attain a knowledge of God. [6]

What Gregory is showing us through his own set of images is that in our relation to God there is a movement from the things we can see and hear and touch—the things about which we believe we know something—and from the words and concepts we use to talk about them and understand them, to the luminous darkness of God where we no longer can know by the positive concepts of our ordinary understanding. The only way to God is the way of negation, the way of saying what God is not. For that way, Gregory uses the image of luminous darkness. I shall talk about the same thing through another image, that of silence. Our images carry us to that luminous darkness as our words carry us to silence. They point us to God. It is not, therefore, a question of our getting beyond the images or the words that we use but a question of our seeing into them.

When we begin to reflect upon things and words and enter into them more deeply, we come before the presence of mystery —the mystery of God, the Being of their being. Things and our words about them have what we might call another side. They not only shine toward us and communicate something of themselves to us, but they also have a side that opens onto God, onto the divine darkness of all being. For that reason, our words about things communicate something more to us than just facts, something more than just bits of knowledge which we can use in different ways. They communicate to us the Being of things; they show us the truth of things in the truth of God. That, I believe, is what Gregory meant when he spoke of the true vision and the true knowledge of that which we seek. Before the Being of all things there can, finally, be only the silence of wonder and thanksgiving for being. That is a silence to which our words about things can direct us as we enter into them and into the intelligibility in which they are grounded. For the Christian believer, who lives in a world of things and words, the journey is to enter into the mystery more deeply and to let things and words communicate the truth in which they are grounded.

To speak in this way is to locate our spirituality even more deeply in what we are as creatures. We are of the earth; we cannot and in fact should not desire to escape from the things of the earth or from our words about those things. To do so would not be to seek the God who makes himself known to us in the things of the world—in Jesus, in bread and wine, and in water. We meet God in the Incarnation of his Word and in the world of things. The Christian believer grows in his spirituality by becoming one who in beholding things beholds what is good and true and beautiful, because he believes all things to be grounded in the goodness, truth, and beauty of God. But he does not stop with their truth, goodness, and beauty as though they were an end. Because they are made in the image of God, men and women are always called to look to the divine ground of things, to enter into that luminous darkness. All images and words direct us through the things of creation to their Creator, just as the humanity of Jesus directs us to its ground, in the eternal Son and Word. The way of negation is not a way of forgetting or denying; it is a way of recalling and affirming.

4

To Speak to God

In all probability there is no area of the Christian life about which so much has been written as about prayer, and much of it, unfortunately, is not always helpful to those of us who find ourselves at the beginning point in the life of prayer. Many of us continue to feel frustrated or guilty because we do not seem to be praying in what we might think of as the right way. We need, however, to think about prayer much more personally, drawing out of our own experience of trying to pray. Praying is not an activity most of us find easy, but it is one we know to be necessary as we stumble about on our own spiritual pilgrimage. And indeed, we shall all probably continue to stumble about for the rest of our lives. One thing absolutely certain about prayer is that we shall never reach the point where we can relax and say, "Now I know how to pray and I needn't work at it any longer."

What are we attempting to do when we pray? The theme I have developed thus far has been to show the way in which our words communicate something to us and to others, as they enable us to understand something of the world in which we live. As images, our words point us in the direction of the ground of all things—to God. When we pray we also use words; we speak in one fashion or other to God. We might even say that we carry on a conversation both with ourselves and with him. And it is important, I believe, to recognize both sides of that conversation: In prayer we are talking to ourselves as well as to God. To deny that is to deny an important part of the process of praying. Why that is true will be developed later, but first a distinction is necessary.

There are basically two kinds of prayer with which most Christian people are familiar. The first is the public prayer of the church: the liturgy that is used in the celebration of the Eucharist as that liturgy has developed in different ways over the centuries. In addition, there is what we call private prayer: our stumbling through words as we pray for or about something that concerns us. These are the kinds of praying from which all of us begin. What is important to recognize is that both arise out of a similar source, what I should call the experience of Christian people. The prayer of the church arises out of the common experience of the body of the faithful, out of all that the community has known and loved, suffered and feared through many centuries of being a community that believes in Jesus Christ. That common experience has even deeper roots in the history of the people of the Old Covenant. To read the Psalter in public prayer and to pray the great prayer of thanksgiving in the Eucharist is to be joined to a common history and experience of many centuries. They are the public memory of the people of God, for the words of our corporate prayer are the way in which God's people have sought to give expression to their most important concerns and to express their thanksgiving to God for his act of redemption in their history. In a similar way, the words we use in our private prayers arise out of our experience of God's redemptive work in our own history. This has been so in my life as I have tried to live it, with all its complexities, problems, and joys, for it is in that life that I have experienced God's gracious presence to me as he has forgiven my sins and led me on to new possibilities of grace. Each of us has his own history, and it is out of the experience of God in that history that we pray. Just as our words about God arise out of a common tradition of human experience, and just as they point beyond themselves to the mystery of God, so our words to God arise out of our public and private experience, and they, too, point us to God.

As with so many words which we use when we speak of the Christian life, the word *experience* has a very complex history and a variety of meanings. For many, it is used simply to mean something personal and private, as when we say, for example, "My experience of the matter has been this." Because it is personal and private, an experience is frequently thought of as subjective and more emotional than otherwise. Hence, when we speak in the area of religion about an experience of God or of any other nonworldly reality, we usually mean a private and particular relationship to something else, a relationship which, because it is so subjective, cannot be communicated in ordinary language. Of course, this is not a wrong use of the word *experience*, but if that is the only sense in which the word is used theologically, it can be somewhat dangerous. What is intended here by the word is much broader than that. I shall use the term to talk about an essentially knowing relation that we may have, either individually or corporately, with something other than ourselves, something which stands over against us as another and of which we must take account in some way. Experience in this sense always involves two poles or dimensions of reality— myself and another; therefore, it implies some kind of emotional and intellectual structure which can be analyzed. Experience, then, involves responding and acting, receiving and giving, myself and another. Experience is an active process in which I act toward something else which also acts toward me; it is not passive receiving. To have an experience of a table, for example, is to be confronted by another object to which I make a certain kind of structured response and which, in turn, even at a very minimal level, gives and receives something from me. We stand in a certain kind of relationship to things other than ourselves whenever we make a judgment about what the thing is and begin that complicated process of naming it. What we have, then, is a process of communication between two realities in which both have an effect upon the other with different degrees of reciprocity. We can see this process most clearly when we experience the reality of another person who consciously and intentionally enters into relationship with us, but it can also be seen, as I have suggested earlier, in a relationship with any created being.

The problem for religious language, of course, begins when we speak of an experience of God. The kind of relationship we have with God as an unseen reality is different from the relationship we have with a table or another person. The content of the reality we experience when we talk about God is different because it comes to us in another way. There are many different ways in which theologians have attempted to show how it is possible for us to experience the reality of that which we call God. Here I want only to suggest one way in which we can speak of an experience of God as it relates to prayer. In prayer we believe that we enter into a relationship with God which we call an experience of God. As Christians, we would want to say that our prayer arises out of the experience of one central event in our lives, an event we continue to experience throughout our lives. That event is what we call salvation, and by salvation we mean a structured event we can characterize in certain definite ways. Speaking of that event in theological language, the Christian says that the event which is central to his experience of God is God's act of redemption in history and his calling of a people to be signs to the world of his saving activity. That act of redemption, which in the Old Testament is shown to us through the history of Israel and the witness of the Law and the prophets, is focused and made concrete and personal in that one event which is central for the Christian, namely, God's act in Jesus Christ. In that act we experience God's will for us, and God's will meets us in our act of corporate and personal prayer. Just as there is a reality with which we must deal in our thinking, so there is a reality with which we must deal when we pray.

In the public liturgy of the Christian church as it has developed over the centuries, the reality we experience is given a clear structure. In the reading and preaching of the word of God the church recalls how God has acted throughout history in order to redeem men and women and call to himself a holy people; in the great prayer of thanksgiving, the church gives thanks for God's continuing act of creation and redemption culminating in the event of Jesus Christ and the presence of his Spirit among us. In recounting that mystery the church remembers the Lord's death in the breaking of bread until he comes again and gives thanks in the offering of praise and thanksgiving. In the Holy Communion the church experiences now that communion with God in Christ which will finally be fulfilled when God is all in all. The experience of salvation in Christ, as it is expressed in the corporate prayer of the church, involves, then, three essential actions: the contemporizing or recalling now of the act of God in our lives through our giving thanks and our waiting in hope for that which is yet to be fulfilled and accomplished in us and in the world. What is at the center of the church's prayer, the experience out of which it arises, is the person Jesus Christ. For this reason we pray in the Holy Spirit of God because it is by the Spirit that we are made able to recall the event of Christ as a present reality and to live in the hope of future glory. The Christian community is that people who have experienced salvation in Jesus Christ, who continue to experience it, and who experience the hope which that salvation brings. The experience of salvation, as the church witnesses to it in prayer, is a public event in space and time and one which is expressed in language that seeks to communicate meaning not only to the lives of individuals but to the historical process as well. The church, in its public prayer, meets and is met by the reality of the will of God made known in Jesus Christ.

In the same way, the prayers that we say alone when we try to communicate to God our needs and joys arise out of that same experience of God's will made known to us in Jesus Christ. That is the experience of salvation which is at the center of all praying. It is much more difficult, however, to speak of personal prayer in this way, because such prayer involves us in private rather than public history. Each of us brings to our experience of salvation in Christ, as we do to our experience of any other person, our own history, in which we have learned how we are being transformed by the Spirit of God. It is always out of my life, out of all its complexities and ambiguities, that I pray. Therefore, to speak about personal prayer is always to speak about myself and to try to communicate in public language what I have experienced in my private history. To speak of God in any form, even in the most abstract theological propositions, involves the speaker in spiritual autobiography, but this is even more evident when we speak of our private life of prayer. And yet we must do precisely that because our private life of prayer, if it is to communicate reality, must arise out of the public and historic experience of the same event, Jesus Christ. That is what

I hope to show in what I have to say about personal prayer as speaking to God.

For most of us, the area out of which we become most conscious of our need to pray and from which we begin, even though we may find many other ways to pray, is the need to discover in our lives what the will of God may be for us and for those whom we love. What I—and I believe many others—can recognize in the history of my attempts at prayer is that I began (and to a considerable extent still continue) to pray for myself and others in terms of telling God what he ought to do. The words of my prayers are the kind that I use when I try to tell something to someone else. If, for example, I believe I need something, my first reaction is to tell someone what I believe I need. On the other hand, if someone comes to me with a problem, my first reaction is to tell him what he ought to do or what he needs to do. And I find myself quite frequently doing the same thing with God. I tell him what would be good for me and for others. Mostly I think of this as the wrong way to pray. Obviously, I ought not to be telling God what to do; to do so is theologically wrong and practically absurd. Yet, when I reflect on what I am doing when I pray in that way, I become aware that something rather significant may be going on. From that way of praying, I believe, two very important things about prayer can be seen, things which remain throughout all of our spiritual pilgrimage.

First, through the process of telling God what is good for me or for someone else, I do in fact begin to see more clearly for myself what the truth of the matter is. I have discovered this in times of great personal need, when I have found myself asking God for a particular thing, knowing that the way in which I was trying to pray was not the best way to pray, but at the same time knowing that for that particular time in my life it was the only way in which I could pray. When we are very much caught up in the emotion of a situation, frequently the only thing we can do is ask for something. Suppose, for example, I am praying for someone I love who is in great pain. My feelings can be very strong that the person I love ought not to be suffering so, and I pray that he may be relieved from the pain. That is a very simple and direct act, one we should never want to lose from our praying. The simple and direct act of petition must always be at the center of prayer, because it is an acknowledgment that God is the Lord of all life. In a similar way, when I want something very badly and really do believe it would be good for me to have it, I pray for it; I ask God to give it to me, as when we say in the Lord's Prayer, "Give us this day our daily bread." This way of speaking is not to be dismissed simply as selfishness (although it can be that), for what can and usually does happen if we persist in our praying is that in asking for what we believe we need we become more and more able to be shown what in truth we do need. We begin to reach the point where the emotional need out of which we began to pray becomes informed by a deeper recognition of the truth of the situation. In other words, we become able to see the emotional need in the larger context of our lives or the life of someone we love. That is something more than simply getting rid of the emotional need or of seeing it simply as wrong; it is a way of dealing with the need honestly and seriously. In the prayer that I offer I sometimes discover that I am being offered myself, and that is to begin the way of transformation. To put the matter in another way, it is to learn that we can pray only in the Spirit of God.

To learn that we can pray only in the Spirit redeems our prayers from being simply a way of talking to ourselves. A very important part of our education and growth as spiritual persons is our learning to deal with all dimensions of ourselves honestly and openly, and that includes our emotional needs and desires as well as our daily bread. I come to God with definite emotions, needs, confusions, and complexities. They are aspects of what I am; they make me a person; and they cannot simply be done away with. Along with everything else that makes me a person, these aspects, too, must be transformed by grace. That means I must learn to see them in the totality of my life—in how I relate to other people and to God. That is the working out of my vocation as a Christian. When I pray, I am coming before God, and that "I" means all of me as one who is open to the possibility of grace. My hope as a person who prays is that someday every area of my life will be open to divine presence, that there will be no closed doors, and that all will have been transformed. But we know ourselves now as persons with many conflicting desires. Now we can only see the beginning of that final hope in the way in which we ask for that which we believe we need, in the words of petition which we speak to God.

The process of transformation, then, is the second thing about prayer that we can begin to see as we reflect upon what we are doing when we ask for something. The person, the one who prays "I need this," is transformed. Here again it is necessary to speak out of one's personal history, out of the various places in which one has found oneself. Out of my own need or out of my concern for another, I ask God for something that seems very important to me. In doing that I discover that one of three things can happen. What I have asked for is not given to me, or it can be given to me in a different way than I had asked, or (sometimes the most terrifying of all) it is given to me as I have asked for it. All of us have known each of those possibilities at various times as a consequence of our praying, and each one of them requires us, if we are to continue in the life of prayer, to ask ourselves what that means for our spirituality. It is, I believe, the most crucial point in our prayer life. Anyone can ask for something, either for himself or for another; the crisis comes after the request has been made, for then we must face reality. To pray out of my own need is essential if I am to pray at all. If prayer stops there, however, I should end up talking to myself; I should end up in the "I" out of which I pray and not move beyond it. As I pointed out earlier, the experience out of which I pray involves something more than myself and my needs.

In our ordinary contact with the world around us, we know there is something other than ourselves. There is a table or a chair that I can bump against; there is another person who has a will of his own. I must take that something else into account if I am to go on living. In our prayer life, that something else is what we call God's will for us, that will which we experience in God's act in Jesus Christ. For the Christian that will is reality; it is the fact of the matter. That will, which we experience in the public and historic event of Jesus Christ, is what makes the difference between prayer and fantasy, for to pray is to meet the reality of God. At that point we can stop praying and withdraw from that reality into ourselves, or we can go on into the mystery of that will for us. As our thinking about things can point us to the reality of God if we go on in our thinking, so too can our praying. Something of what it means to go on in prayer I shall suggest in the next chapter.

5

Meeting God in Prayer

The point of crisis in the prayer of petition or intercession begins when we discover that we are confronted by the will of God. It is a perfectly natural thing to request something from someone else; we do it all the time in our relations with one another. A child, for example, soon learns that not everything it wants will be given, and we adults learn the same thing in our daily contacts with one another. We deal with that reality in different ways. In fact, one of the ways in which we grow into responsible adulthood is by learning to deal with the will of others through the discovery that we shall not get everything we want.

In prayer, however, the matter is more difficult. If we are not given what we ask for by a parent or friend, we can, at least, be given an explanation. Even about those things which seem to happen to us by blind chance, some natural explanation can be found for what has happened. But in our dealing with God, no such obvious explanations are given to us. God does not speak to us in that direct way. (He may, indeed, speak to us in other than direct ways, but the hearing of that requires that we have learned to hear him, and so is much further along the way.)

There is a second difficulty. Most of us have been taught through Scripture and public worship to believe that God is a good and loving father who cares for us, and so we often find ourselves asking how he can refuse what we in all sincerity ask. Why does God allow someone we love to suffer great pain? Often we Christians who have become accustomed to pious explanations of human pain and suffering can obscure the seriousness of that question for ourselves as well as for others who are not yet believers. It is, however, a question which has been put powerfully to a great many people in our time because of the horrors that have been inflicted on them and others: the extermination of the Jews under the Nazis, the prison camps in Russia, and the racial and political hatred we have known in this country. How can God be called good when such things happen? Many of us know that question in our own pain and suffering, and sometimes we lose faith because of it. And yet, the Christian knows that many have discovered the deepest resources of their faith through the suffering, pain, and horror which can strike people. How can one understand prayer as meeting the will of God in every circumstance of life? That is a serious and fundamental question.

Another difficulty, and one which is much harder to state, is the most crucial of all. When we were children it was easy for us to understand why we could ask favors of God; we did it in the same way that we asked favors of our parents. Children are accustomed to doing that; adults, however, are not. As we grow older and become more responsible for our own lives, we learn not to ask favors of others. We are expected to accomplish things for ourselves and to become independent of favors. Once again, we who are conditioned by a certain piety can obscure from ourselves the seriousness of the difference that makes. What we should not think of doing elsewhere in our lives, we do in our prayers, and that can produce a serious dichotomy in our lives. The non-Christian can ask us in all seriousness: If you are an adult and responsible for your own life (and that is a good thing, because it is the foundation of morality), why then is God necessary at all? To face that question honestly and seriously is to realize why prayer is at the heart of Christian belief. A person may believe in God as a philosophic or scientific principle, but does he pray to him? That is the deep meaning of faith in God.

In what follows I shall speak from the experience of prayer to the experience of prayer, in order that we might see how we deal with some of those difficulties ourselves, for in those difficulties is raised, for us who pray, the question of the will of God.

Let us recall the times when we have asked something directly of God, and consider what happened. There are three possibilities. We can believe that God has answered our prayer, that he has not, or that he has answered it in a way different from that we had expected. What is important here, however, is that we say we believe that God has responded in a certain way. There is, after all, no way in which we can prove to the satisfaction of ourselves or anyone else that things would not have worked out in the same way had we not prayed. What does or does not happen in a concrete situation as a result of prayer is not subject to proof. That our prayers have consequences for ourselves and others is a matter of belief. We believe that God acts in our lives, and only in the context of that belief can we speak of prayer as the place in which we meet God's will for us.

The context of belief in which we pray and in which we are met by the will of God means that there is a situation of trust or confidence in Another. But trust and confidence in Another are not things that simply happen, nor are they usually total and complete. Anyone who has entered seriously into prayer and who has, therefore, been met by God, knows that he is required to grow in trust and confidence, to grow in the belief that God acts in his life. Many times we fail in trust and confidence, and each of us can recall those times in life when we have cried out in despair because we believed ourselves deserted by God. On the other hand, if despite those times we have gone on and continued to pray, we can see how we have grown and been transformed. There are two examples which, I believe, can help us see more clearly what has happened and continues to happen when we pray. Both are drawn from that area which is most familiar to us, namely, our relationships with other people. As examples, they are limited, but they point in a direction where we can begin to see more clearly what it is to be met by God and to respond in trust and confidence to the will which meets us.

The trust and confidence that a small child has in his parents can help us to understand the most basic relationship we have with God. A small baby comes to life surrounded by the love of parents. The child is fed, held, and loved from the beginning, and the trust which develops and grows in that child can be called a natural response in the sense that it develops unreflectively. The child depends upon its parents for life and does not have to think about what it gets. Only much later in life does the child begin to reflect on that relationship and to see what was involved—both the strength and the failure, for neither parents nor children are perfect in love. But at the beginning, this relationship of child to parents is simply something that happens to the child and makes him live; it is fundamental and as out of the child's control as being born.

Something very similar happens between us and God. To the believer, God is simply there in the beginning. In an earlier chapter we have seen how this was the experience of Israel in the Old Testament. Israel came to understand God as creator through its experience of him in its history and in reflection upon what that relationship meant for its own vocation. Moreover, in the Old Testament account of creation there is no attempt to explain God or justify belief in him. He is simply there, in the beginning. As men and women begin to reflect upon their world and their history, other questions arise which must be dealt with in a different way, but in the beginning there is God. He stands to us in a way that we can partially understand through the relationship of child and parent. We grow in our relationship of trust and confidence with the God who is there, just as children grow in trust and confidence with their parents. We put both of them to the test, not so much to test their trustworthiness but to discover how much room we have for our growth. In the religious experience of many people (although, of course, not of all), only the most radical and violent act can destroy that relationship of trust and confidence, that belief that God acts for our good. When that happens, as we know from the spiritual literature of many centuries, a person can be thrown into a fundamental despair which leads to death, or he can discover, precisely in his sense of abandonment by God, a new spiritual pilgrimage. The story of Israel in the Old Testament and of the Jewish people in modern times bears witness to both those possibilities. For many Jews the Holocaust in Europe destroyed all belief in God's care for his people, but many others found in that devastation a renewed awareness of the depth of their vocation to be God's people. The Christian who hears the cry of Jesus on the cross, ''My God, my God, why have you forsaken me?'' cannot doubt for himself the terrifying alternatives of death or life. Indeed, what makes the alternative of death and life possible for the believer is his fundamental relationship to the God who has met him in prayer and elsewhere in his life. We can only believe ourselves to be abandoned and forsaken by someone who has been known to be there all along.

What I am describing here as a fundamental sense of the presence of God means that human beings simply as human beings are called to live in the relationship of sonship to God. This relationship to God is one which we can reject only by an active repudiation of it, by a total turning into self and away from God. Thomas Aquinas, in a striking image, says that to reject the grace of God is as though we were to close our eyes to the midday sun although even then we should continue to live in that light.[1] That many people do reject the light within which the Christian believes every person exists, and that many others do not know the Christian name for the light in which they live, is obviously true. From both facts arises the Christian imperative to preach that Name to those who do not yet know it and to discover for themselves the truth in the other names by which that light is known. But the light we believe is there in the beginning, and the response to it, in whatever form, is that created spirituality of our humanity within which prayer is possible.

The second example, drawn also from our experience of loving and trusting others, grows out of the first. There comes a time in the lives of most of us when reflection upon what it is to love and trust another person becomes necessary. The act of reflecting may arise in relation to our parents, when we discover the strengths and the limitations of that love, or, more frequently, it may arise through the discovery that we love and trust in another person. In other words, what happens to most of us is that we fall in love. There is that flash of joy and surprise when we realize, that is, when we consciously know, that we can and do love another person. There are many forms which that realization can take, and it is neither possible nor necessary to examine each here. As far as I can see, however, there is a basic pattern to all of them. What happens is that we are drawn to another by beauty. It may be beauty of physical form or beauty of spirit, but another person strikes us with beauty and we fall in love. To fall in love, however, is only the beginning. We must grow in love and trust if we are to go on loving another person.

For most of us, what falling in love means is that we begin to make very tentative movements toward the other person in order to see whether what we have seen as beautiful is really the case. There are, of course, many different things that can happen, including disappointment and failure. Hopefully, what happens is that we grow into a new and radically important relationship through which, over many years, we learn to believe in one another more and more deeply. It is not just that we learn to trust what another person may say or do, for, given the frailty and sin of human beings, those things may be very ambiguous. Rather, we learn to believe in what we call the reality of another person. To say to another person, "I trust you and I believe in you," does not mean that we always understand or approve of what is said or done. It means that we have come to believe and are growing in the belief that the person acts out of a center of heart, mind, and will that is worthy of trust. This is a growing and transforming process, and it requires the discipline of self-honesty and the discipline of reflection upon what it is to love and trust another human being.

To be met by the reality of heart, mind, and will in another person is to discover in ourselves a new level of trust and belief, for it requires that we ask ourselves whether we shall go on or whether we shall turn back into ourselves. For example, the disagreements that occur between two people who love one another can be trivial or serious, but they give rise to the necessity of asking, "What do I trust, and how shall I react to the disagreement?" Does disagreement give rise to radical distrust, that kind of distrust because of which the relationship is ended? Or am I still able to say to someone, however weakly and hesitantly, that despite our disagreement I believe in him or her and trust the integrity of his or her will, heart, and mind in this matter? To trust another in that way does not come spontaneously; it arises out of a long discipline of love, for so to trust is not an easy thing. It is a discipline which begins with another who was there in the beginning and who, perhaps in some new form, has been discovered again. And as we well know, there are times when, through weakness or self-will, we do draw back into ourselves, and there is a radical break which can be healed only by an equally radical act of forgiveness and reconciliation. If the basic relationship is serious and strong enough, then we are able to find a way for reconciliation and continue to grow in trust.

What I am suggesting in this familiar example is that this is what happens between God and us. Through prayer, as we are met by his will, we do grow in trust and we are transformed in our need. There is, however, more to the matter than that. The process of our transformation is not just that we learn to accept another heart, mind, and will in a passive and childlike manner. In order for me to be a person who is serious in his relationships with others, I must also learn to accept what is legitimate in myself. No more in prayer than in any other area of my life can I forget the personal history out of which I pray. That history has formed me as a person. We know from our experience that we are able to love others and to accept the authority of their love in our lives only when we have a mind, heart, and will of our own. To say "I love you" to another person is to speak out of a personal center which has its own history of strengths and weaknesses. What we see in Christ, for example, is one who was able to love others neither by imposing his will upon them nor by allowing them to impose their will on him. He could accept others and their will for him out of his own strength and as his vocation rather than by passive submission. His freedom to love others, even those who put him to death, derived from his knowledge of who he was and what he was called to do. The transformation which takes place in us through our being met by God is the discovery of who we are and what we are called to be. Transformation through prayer is to be able to say that I, in my own heart, mind, and will, accept that which I have been called to be and to do. Only in this sense can the trust and love which we have for another person enable us to become free to love others. When I am able to act toward others out of a freedom to be who I am, then I am not just a passive recipient

for whatever may happen to me. That is the freedom we learn
(or fail to learn) through meeting the heart, mind, and will of
another.

In prayer we speak words to God out of our need, and those
words point beyond themselves. They point to the need that is
to be transformed, and they point to the God who speaks to us
and who transforms our need into the freedom to love and to
trust him. Because our words point to the word that God speaks
to us, they direct us to him who wills to be our savior; they direct
us beyond our need to our salvation. The word that he speaks
enables us to speak and centers us in him.

6

Being Centered in God

Up to this point we have been considering how we discover our identity and our center as persons through thinking and praying. As we speak about God in the language of theology, we discover that our words, arising out of our experience point us to the mystery of God as the ground of intelligibility in things. In a similar way, the words we speak to God in prayer arise out of need and out of meeting with another will that calls us. We began, that is to say, with the words that we speak, and we have seen how, for those who believe, those words are not an end in themselves. Their end is in the God who speaks his word to us in Jesus Christ. That he speaks his word to us is what makes the difference between being centered in ourselves and being centered in God. For the Christian that difference is crucial, because we believe that we are truly persons only as we are centered in God. God centers us in the word that he speaks to us.

When Christians speak about the word of God, they can mean many different things. In an earlier chapter we saw the importance of the word *logos* in the theological tradition about Jesus Christ. Frequently the expression also refers to Holy Scripture, not in the sense that God actually wrote down the words of the Bible but in the sense that those human words bear witness in a unique way to God's work and will in human history. We also say that a sermon can be the word of God to a particular congregation. All these meanings have an underlying sense that can help us understand what it means to say that God speaks his word to us when in our thinking and praying we speak about him and to him in our words. That underlying sense is God's will for our salvation and his accomplishment of his will in our lives. As I said earlier, our experience of salvation in Jesus Christ is the source for all that we do as Christian people. That experience is not something private and internal. It is the experience of something public and historic had by a community. We need now to go more deeply into that experience in order to see how God's word to us forms our words by centering our lives in him.

Thinking and praying both involve a process of working things through. Some of us can see that process more clearly in our thinking because it is through the process of thinking that we work things out in our ordinary lives. To think through a question means to work toward a goal and to discover the solution to a problem. There is an end in view, although at the beginning it may not be clear what that end is. In thinking through a question, therefore, we discover that we have to be open to new data which may change our direction. The new data that emerges along the way interprets what we have known before and puts it in a new perspective. It enables us to see the problem in a new way and to discover that the end may not be precisely where we thought it would be. Although many of us might not so readily recognize it (I write personally here, because it is one of my own difficulties in the life of prayer), the same process takes place in our praying as we pray through a particular problem. In that process we are confronted by the will of God. God makes his will known to us in the process of our struggle to pray and to find the words in which to pray. Finding the words in which to pray is as important in praying as finding the words in which to express our thoughts. In both thinking and praying we enter into a mystery, and we carry through until we reach the end.

For the person who thinks or prays seriously, the end of the process is always a new beginning, not the solution to a problem to which *finis* can then be written. The end of the process of thinking and praying illuminates everything that has gone before; it puts the starting point itself into a new perspective, showing facets or dimensions of it that before had not been obvious. If we remember *who* is doing the thinking and praying, we can perhaps see this aspect of both more clearly. I think through a problem or I pray about a situation, and the I that thinks or prays obviously does not remain static in the process. At each step of the way and at the end, I am faced with a new perception of reality with which I must deal and which I must encompass into the whole of my life. I see myself in a new way because of the end that I have reached; I can never be the same person again. In this process, what does it mean to say that God's word meets us and centers us as persons?

What Christians traditionally have called the word of God that meets us and centers us is revelation and, most especially, God's act of self-disclosure in Jesus Christ. We believe that Jesus Christ shows us the truth about God's will for us and the truth about us and our world. That truth is the end of our thinking and praying, because it is saving truth. In other words, we have been concerned in previous chapters to see how we become centered as persons through our thinking and praying, and to see how those two fundamental activities are related to each other. The words we speak in both activities enable us to find out the truth about ourselves and the truth about the world in which we live. In the words of our thinking and praying, we try to express to ourselves, to others, and to God what it is we need, believe, feel, or understand about a particular situation. But the Christian is not finally interested in that kind of personal-centeredness if that is all that can be said about us. The non-Christian, or one who is not a believer at all, could make much the same kind of statement about thinking or about that activity which might be called reflection or meditation. Reflection and meditation are by no means activities limited to Christian believers; they are to be found among those of other religious traditions as well as among those who are not specifically or positively involved in a religious tradition. For us, however, who believe in the God who is the Father of Jesus Christ and who calls us to himself through his Holy Spirit, that kind of psychological description, as good as it may be, does not go far enough. We believe not only that we discover our own center through our thinking and praying but also that in those two activities God meets us and centers us in himself. In the word which he speaks to us he informs our words. To believe that makes a world of difference, for it is to believe that God is the center of our lives. If we are to move beyond a description of our praying and thinking as activities in which we only discover something about ourselves and our world, then we must consider how God is our center, and only as he is our center can we truly be persons. That is the message of the gospel.

One way in which we can begin to see how God is our center and how he centers us in himself is to look at that central Christian doctrine which speaks most clearly to what we believe about God and ourselves, namely, the doctrine of the incarnation of the word of God in Jesus of Nazareth. We believe that in the historical person Jesus Christ there is a meeting of humanity and divinity: He who is human in all those respects that are true about us is united with the eternal word of God. Furthermore, as Christians we believe that the meeting and the union between his humanity and the *logos* of God is so fundamental, so deep and all-encompassing, that the only way we have to describe it in our language is to say that it is a personal unity between man and God. To say anything less is to say something less than the truth about the one whom we call Savior and Lord. To say that the unity of God and man in Jesus Christ is something less than personal is to deny either the fullness and completeness of his humanity or the fullness and completeness of his divinity. What we want to say about Jesus, because we know him as Savior and Lord, is that he is one who acts and speaks out of a personal center that is neither divided against itself nor something less than that which we are aware of in ourselves. Therefore, if we are to be true to the way in which the Christian community has experienced Jesus as Savior and Lord, we cannot say, for example, that at one time Jesus spoke only our human words and at another time God's words. Nor can we say that at one time he acted as a human being and that at another time he acted as God. Every word he spoke and every act of his came out of a center which was one, a unity. When Jesus speaks and acts in the gospels with authority, the I out of which he speaks and acts is the personal unity of the eternal word of God and a human mind, heart, and will. Only as that personal unity can he be called our Savior and Lord. Anything else would be mockery either of God or of us.

That is the doctrine the church has expressed in its creeds. Something more needs to be said, however, about the mystery of that personal union in order that we may see how his personal unity is the truth about us, the pattern for our transformation, and not just a formal or abstract doctrine. But it must be very clear that we cannot attempt to give some kind of psychological description of the interior life of Jesus himself, for we cannot penetrate that mystery. When such an attempt has been made by theologians and others, the result has been either to deny his personal unity or to deny the fullness and completeness of his human mind, will, and heart. We cannot engage in that kind of speculation about the interior life of Jesus, because we can only approach him, so to speak, from our side, from the experience we have of him as Savior and Lord. In that experience he presents himself to us as one who is the personal unity of God and man.

The mystery of Christ's personal unity as God and man, as we experience it, is important for two reasons. First, it enables us to say something of importance about him as the revelation of God to us, as the one who speaks God's word to us. Second, it enables us to say something of importance about our salvation in him. Jesus Christ, as he is remembered by the church in Holy Scripture, had a human history. He grew, developed, and changed. He underwent temptation. He even struggled to accept the vocation given to him in the cross. All that is evident in Scripture, and when that personal history of Jesus Christ is forgotten, as it sometimes is by Christians, the forgetting of it can only lead to a false doctrine about Christ and to a dangerous form of spirituality. To forget that Christ shares in our humanity totally and completely, to forget that he has a human history, is to turn him into some kind of quasi-human figure who was simply pretending to share with us in all that it is to be human, and that can provide us with an excuse to avoid the explanation of our own humanity. The unity of the *logos* with the humanity of Jesus requires us to take our humanity, our human history, with ultimate seriousness, for it is our human history which is redeemed in Christ. At the same time, however, it must be said clearly that both the Christian experience of Christ and the credal formulations of the church have insisted that Jesus the man did not grow into divinity—whatever that might mean. He did not become the eternal Logos during the course of his human history. What he was seen to be by his disciples in his resurrection from the dead, and how he is known by us now, he was from the beginning. Thus, the important question for us, who experience him as Savior and Lord, is how we are to approach that unity of humanity and divinity in terms of the human history of Jesus. How can that human history, as moving and edifying as it certainly is, be distinguished from the personal history of any other great figure? All that he said could have been said by others, and there are many reports of miracle workers who did the things Jesus is reported to have done. Indeed, in all probability what he did and said would not have been remembered had it not been for that one significant event that put all his deeds and words into a completely new perspective. The event was that he was raised from the dead and that those who believed in him (even though they may not have been able to say why they did) were transformed by the power of his Spirit. That event enabled them to see that everything he had said and done in the human history which they had known had arisen out of his unity with the one he called his father. Who Jesus was for his disciples in the first century and who he is for those who believe in him now is shown in the power of his resurrection from the dead, for that power transforms the lives of those who believe in him. In that event, he is the revelation of God to us. When we confess that Jesus Christ is the revelation of God to us, we confess that the revelation is not simply in what he said and did but in the truth he declares about us and about the God whose being he shares and whom he represents. He speaks the word of God to us by being who he is—the personal unity of God and man. He shows us the nature of God as the one who calls all human beings to himself and who transforms them by his Holy Spirit, and he shows us our nature as those who are called to God.

Approaching the mystery of the person of Christ in this way can tell us something important about the way in which Jesus Christ centers us as human beings in God. The resurrection of Christ from the dead is the event through which everything else about him becomes of saving significance for us because it gives to his whole life the power to transform us. That he transforms us is something known to Christians in many different ways. The power by which he transforms us we call the Holy Spirit.

No area of Christian belief is more difficult to talk about than the doctrine of the Holy Spirit. While all Christians are to some degree aware of the presence and power of the Spirit in their lives, most of us find it very difficult to say what we mean by that presence. It seems to be much easier for us to speak of the work of Christ in his death on the cross and his resurrection from the dead than it is for us to speak of the presence of the Holy Spirit as that which transforms us. Perhaps that is why so many Christians today feel uncomfortable with the pentecostal movement in the church, for those who call themselves Pentecostals are attempting to give a fuller expression to that presence and power than many of us feel comfortable with. On the other hand, for all of us who would call ourselves Christians and who, therefore, confess a faith in the God who is Father, Son, and Holy Spirit, it is essential to recognize what that presence and power is. Indeed, the neglect of the doctrine of the Holy Spirit in the theology of the Western church has been an unfortunate consequence of the way in which our theology has developed in other areas. We have placed so great an emphasis on our redemption from sin through the cross that we have often failed to see the equal importance of our transformation by the power of the Holy Spirit. Many would now agree that the most important theological task of our time is to regain, in all its theological, liturgical, and spiritual depth, a sense of the presence of the Holy Spirit as a transforming power.

One way in which we know that transforming power is in what happens when, in our human words, we struggle to pray and think. As we have seen, both praying and thinking are a journey of discovery, a process of working through a situation and of coming to a new place in which the will of God and the intelligibility of things become clearer and more compelling for us. In our thinking and in our praying we are met by God, and we are met in such a way that what we have been and what we are struggling to become are expressed in the word of truth we speak about ourselves and about the God who meets us. To pray through a situation or to think through a question means to discover the words which must be spoken and to be able to speak them.

When I pray, I am trying to discover how the petition I want to make can be spoken. I am praying that a person may be healed or that something may be done. What is it that I am asking for? What is the content of my prayer? Because we are human we must communicate in language, and we seek to express the content of our prayers in the words through which we attempt to say what we mean to say. We do this in both public and private prayer, for the word which is spoken is the means through which the truth is spoken. This is not some form of magic, as though God responds only when the right word is spoken by us. It is, rather, a process of communication by which we say what we believe to be the case, and in saying it we believe we are heard. The word which is spoken from us to God expresses all that we mean to say about a situation insofar as we can understand it and present it to him. But there is another side to this process. In order to speak the word of truth about any situation, I must have heard the word of truth spoken to me. The word I speak is the word I have heard. To discover the word of truth in prayer or in thinking is to discover God's will for us and his presence to all things.

What I mean can be put very simply. It is the difference between saying "My will be done" and saying "Your will be done." To say "My will be done" is to speak the word of pride, because it is to refuse to acknowledge another. Already we have seen something of what that difference means when it takes place between one person and another. Carried to its end, it is the failure of love and trust. On the other hand, to be able to say to another person "Your will be done" is not to cower before an arbitrary decree given by someone else. To acknowledge the presence of another in whom I believe and in whom I trust, is to be a free person. To be a free person is to be able to recognize the authority of another person in one's life, not as a slave acknowledges the authority of a master but as a lover acknowledges the authority of the one he loves. To say "Your will be done" is a free act of love, and the person who is able to do that is one who knows where his center is. He is free to speak the word of truth about himself because he has heard it from another. All of us surely know how difficult it is to become that kind of person in our daily lives. In our journey of love with one another, to become that kind of person requires of us a discipline through which we learn to trust and believe in others. It is, however, the pattern for all that we mean when we speak of our transformation by the Spirit of God. In so many tentative and halting ways, we learn through the life of prayer what it is to be met by Another, and to trust that Other by whom we are met. That is our education into God, or, as we can now call it, our transformation by the Spirit. In a tentative way now and with final thanksgiving at the end of our lives, to be able to say to God, "Your will be done," means that we have become able to speak the word of truth about everything that has happened to us in all the places from which we have come, and to look in trust toward that which may yet be the will of the God whom we have come to know. In other words, to be centered in God and, therefore, to be able to speak the word of thanksgiving, "Your will be done," is something much more than accepting something given to me from outside myself. It is, rather, that my word has been formed by God's word.

Our speaking about God in words ends in the same place, or, rather, with the same word. To speak about the mystery of all being is to discover the word of truth that must be spoken about all that is. What I mean by that can, I believe, be made more clear if we think about the difference between telling a lie and telling the truth. We all tell lies from time to time. But we recognize that there is a difference between making a mistake or simply trying to protect ourselves with an equivocation and those lies which fundamentally distort reality. To lie about who we are and what we are called to become, or to lie about the state of things as that affects others, is of much greater consequence. The radically serious kind of lie is the one which represents a denial of the intelligibility of things and of our ability to know what is true about them. As we saw in an earlier chapter, to think things, to enter into a question, and to express in words the truth of things is a fundamental quality of human spirituality and is the gift of *logos* within us. To lie about the nature of things and their calling into God as the source and end of all created being is to deny both God and ourselves. That kind of lie can be told on many different levels, but basically it represents one thing: a form of denying that there is a truth about us and the world which has an integrity and value that cannot finally be reduced to my own desires and fantasies. Sin has its root in our pride, by means of which we turn everything and everyone into a source for our own gratification. To sin is to use the world for myself and to deny its reality apart from me. To tell a lie is to do the same thing in the life of knowing and thinking. To lie about ourselves and the way in which things are is to deny that there is anything or anyone outside myself which lays upon me the claim of truth. To lie is to reduce the world to my own fantasy. To think, and to struggle to find the words through which I can speak the truth, is the spiritual quality of human beings as human beings. It is by no means a quality had only by those who would call themselves religious and who would identify the truth of things with God. Any human being who seeks to discover and to say what is true is acknowledging and accepting for himself a value beyond himself, which transcends his desires and wishes, and which, indeed, transcends himself. In human history, that truth which transcends us has been called by many different names and has compelled human beings to enter upon many different spiritual pilgrimages. Basically, that truth is what we mean when we speak of reality, what is the case, no matter how much we would prefer it to be otherwise. This truth is the reality to which we must adjust ourselves because it stands over against us and calls us to it. What we as Christians believe is that that reality, that truth which transcends us and calls us to itself, is the God who speaks to us in Jesus Christ and who transforms us in his Spirit. The Christian name for truth is God, and therefore we would want to say that to speak the word of truth is to speak God's word. The word of truth which is spoken, whether it be about such a simple thing as a table or chair or whether it be the more profound truth about another human being, is always an image which points beyond itself to God. In praying we learn by the Spirit to say that the light of God's truth shines in everything that is. To speak that word is to be in the presence of the mystery of God, who is the light of intelligibility in all things and whose will is reality.

To speak the word of truth to God and about him is a pilgrimage of discovery which begins from our need and from our awareness of things and ends with our knowledge of who God is and who we are. To make that pilgrimage requires of us a particular discipline and formation. It is the discipline of learning to hear the word which is spoken to us in Jesus Christ. The word he speaks to us is, as we have seen, the totality of his life, death, and resurrection. That truth is that we, as human beings, as what we are with our own personal histories, are called into a unity of heart, mind, and will with the God who has created us and who calls us to our end. That is the word of truth, spoken to us in the resurrection of Christ, which we must hear and which we must learn to speak ourselves. Sometimes, even now, we are able to hear it and to speak it; the Christian hope is that the whole creation redeemed by the Son and transformed by the Spirit will speak its "Amen" to God. The centering not only of our own lives but also of the whole creation in God is the truth about us which we dimly perceive but for which we live in hope. When the whole creation is so centered, there will only be silence before the mystery of God.

7

The Word of Thanksgiving

In the last chapter, we considered the journey or pilgrimage through which we are transformed by the Spirit and in which we learn to hear the word of truth which is spoken about us in Christ. He is the word of truth about us, and he speaks that word to us in the total event of his life, death, and resurrection from the dead. The truth that he speaks is our hope and, to some degree, a present reality for us. Because we are now able to see, however dimly, what it is to be united to God in Christ, we enter more and more deeply into the pilgrimage to our transformation. What we must now consider, however, is something more of the relationship between the present, in which we are able to catch a glimpse of that unity, and the hope of its fulfillment. I believe that it will be helpful for us to approach that relationship through the word which we speak now in anticipation of the silence of our unity with God—that silence which is the end of our praying and our thinking. The word we speak now is a word of thanksgiving; it anticipates the silence of thanksgiving in God, just as it completes the past out of which it is spoken.

To be on a journey involves two things which are important for us to consider. It means, first of all, that I am coming from someplace. There is something behind me, a past or a place, from which I have come. Second, it means that I am going somewhere. I have a goal or an end in view. When the journey is simply geographical, both the place from which we have come and the place to which we are going are fairly clear and definite. We determine how to get from one place to another place, and we have some idea of what we shall find when we arrive. In what we might call a journey of the mind or spirit, however, things are not so clear and definite. We may know that we are traveling, but it may not be very clear to us where we have come from or where we are going. That we have all come from someplace is, of course, true; that is what I have called our personal histories, that history which contains all our failures and pains as well as our achievements and joys. Most human beings reflect upon their past in some form or another, and so they have some idea of the place from which they have come. They are able to see where they made certain decisions and failed to make others and how the past has brought them to the place where they now are. But when we think about it, we also know that where we are now does not have permanence. The present is soon to be the past, and the decisions which are now made have consequences we cannot yet anticipate. So, even though we may know something of the past from which we have come, we cannot speak about it or analyze it as precisely as we might like.

About the end of our spiritual or mental journeys, however, there is even less that can be understood and spoken of. While we may have a general idea about what we hope will be our goal, we cannot be certain about what we shall find when we arrive, nor can we be certain that the goal we see now will remain unchanged as we move on. One of the interesting, and sometimes frightening, things about journeys of the mind and spirit is the possibility of surprise at the end. Our end is not predetermined, and, of course, every end leads on to new possibilities.

That is all fairly commonplace in the experience of most human beings. There is nothing uniquely Christian or even religious about it. The scholar or scientist, engaged in some form of research, knows that he cannot predetermine where his investigations will lead him, and often he is not even certain about why he began the journey in the first place. Something may have got him started that cannot now be understood or even remembered. The Christian believer, however, does see the journey of heart, mind, and will in a certain light, and that way of seeing does make a difference. We believe ourselves to have come from someplace, and we believe we are headed in a certain direction. We know that we, like any other human being, have no absolute certainty about either the past or the future, but we see both from a perspective made different by the faith we confess. Christians believe that they are called from a past into a future which is characterized for them by the figure of Jesus Christ. The people who believe in Jesus Christ as the one whom God raised from the dead and as the one who is the perfect unity of God and man believe that their end is Christ. Precisely what that may involve we cannot claim to know—at least we do not claim to know it if we are faithful to the words of Paul and of the writer of the Epistles of John. What we confess is not an exact knowledge of our end but a person who is our end. John says we do not know now what we shall be; we know only that we shall be like Christ; and Paul says, in a similar way, that then we shall know as we are known. But to believe that Christ is our end does give us a different way of seeing our past and our future, which enables us to see both in terms of our present.

While on the journey from the past toward a future hope, we live in the present. If we consider it, however, the notion of the present is something very odd. I want to suggest that this oddness is what makes the notion of the present particularly significant for those of us who are Christians. The present is something of a fleeting moment; there is a certain unreality about it, for as soon as we have become aware of it, it has already passed us by. As soon as I am able to speak about the present, it has already become a past which cannot be altered or changed in any way. Similarly, the present is always that upon which the future impinges, and so it can never be grasped or held onto. What we mean when we speak of the present time—whether we speak of a second, a day, a year, or even of a present age—is a fleeting moment between the past and the future. At the same time, however, that fleeting moment of the present is the only reality we have. The past has gone, and it cannot be changed or recaptured; the future is not yet and, since anyone may die in a moment, it may never be. The present is all that there is. The present is where we live and is, therefore, the moment of truth about us. For that reason, the word we speak in the present is the word of truth which says where we have come from, where we hope to go, and where we are now. As we have seen, to pray and to think in such a way that our words become informed by the word God speaks to us in Jesus Christ is to be able to say that God's will be done and that he is the truth of all things. As our words point to the one word which informs and centers them in the reality of God, so also they arise out of the one truly human word which Jesus speaks in his own humanity as he offers himself to the Father. This word is the word we in our humanity speak as we offer ourselves to God in the present moment, the word of the creature to the Creator which draws together and focuses on where we have come from and where we are going. This is the word of thanksgiving: Amen, so be it.

There are many different ways in which we could begin to enter more deeply into what it is to say the word of thanksgiving. I want here to approach the giving of thanks through that particular act which is fundamental to the life of the Christian community, namely, the Eucharist. I have already (in Chapter 4) said something of the Eucharist as the public prayer of the Christian community. There we saw that this sacrament is the act in which the community recalls, through the Spirit, God's act of salvation in Jesus Christ. Now I want to think of the Eucharist as the act which sums up all that can be said about our existence in time and space in the one word of thanksgiving which we speak.

What all Christians believe about the Eucharist is that it is action that recalls to us what God has done in our history and one that makes the past present to us in what we now do. There have been many different ways in the theological and liturgical tradition of describing and defining the way in which God's act of salvation in Jesus Christ is now made present to us. Beneath all those ways, however, is a common theme. For the community which believes that in Jesus Christ God has acted for our salvation, the past is not something gone and forgotten. The past is the history of our relationship with God, the relationship he has established in us in Christ through the Spirit and out of which we have come and through which we have been educated as a people. The Jews in the time of Jesus had—and still have—

as the central event of their life as a people the recalling of the Exodus, that time when God led them out of bondage in Egypt into the promised land. That event formed them as a people with a particular vocation, and the annual recalling of it still remains central to their present existence as a people with a particular vocation. Christians believe that in the Last Supper, Jesus associated the meal he had with his disciples with the event of the Passover and gave it a new meaning—one associated with his own death and the hope of his resurrection. The community which shared in that meal with him believed itself to have been formed by the Holy Spirit into a new community, and so they then, as we now, gathered together in order to make present what was the central event in their experience of salvation, namely, that Christ had been raised from the dead. For every Christian, no matter what his particular tradition, the past is the history of what God has done, and what he is doing now is understood and interpreted in terms of what he has done for us in Jesus Christ. But, we believe, that is not all. Not only do we give thanks in the Eucharist for what God has done for us in the past, but we also declare our hope about what he will do for us in the future. In the word of thanksgiving, which the Eucharist is, the truth about our past and our future is spoken. Jesus, who is the true word about us, because he is God's word to us, is present to us now as the truth about the past and the future. The past and the future are drawn together in the present as that moment of time in which the true word is spoken. That is what centers us as a people. It is the history of our salvation and the promise of our future glory.

For that we give thanks. To see the present as the focus of the past in which we have been saved and of the future in which we shall be transformed means that there is only one word which can be spoken, the word of thanksgiving. That we are able to speak that word and so to acknowledge the gift which is given to us is the work of the Holy Spirit in our lives, transforming us into those who can acknowledge a gift given. Perhaps we can see somewhat more clearly what this means if we reflect upon what it is to acknowledge any gift given to us. The most obvious example of a gift given is that of love itself. Anyone who has known himself or herself to be loved by another person, whether it be by spouse, by parents, or by friends, ought to know that he or she has done nothing to deserve or require the gift that has been given to him. There is, quite literally, nothing that we can do in order to deserve such a gift. This love is something given to us freely and in full recognition of the faults and limitations we may have, or it is not given at all. And we know something of the gift of love, also, from the other side, that is, from the rather incredible fact that we ourselves are able to love others. We love them not because they are without fault but because there is that in them which moves us to give to them the gift of our own love. The love we human beings have for one another is, of course, limited. It can come and go; it can be distorted by our own folly and sinfulness into something else. But in our attempts to grow more into love and to respond more deeply to the love given to us, we learn something of what it is to be given a gift and to give a gift to another. The most important thing we learn in that process is that the only response we can finally make to love given to us or which we hope will be given to the love that we have for others is love itself. That is what it means to say that the word of thanksgiving is the only true word we can speak about ourselves. To say thank you to another for the gift that is given is the free and loving response of a person who is able to receive a gift not through any claim which may be laid upon another but only through an ability to give ourselves to another. When I am able to accept my history with all its complexities and my future with all its uncertainties as that which is loved, then I am able to say thank you to the one who loves me. In that word of thanks my past and my future are brought together and are given over to another as they are, without the necessity of deception, because I might fear that were I truly known I should not be loved. It is that free offering of himself which we believe Jesus does on the cross when he commits his past and his future into the hands of his Father. And we catch a glimpse of his free offering of himself in our own lives when, from time to time, we are able to speak the same word of thanksgiving. We speak to God in prayer and we speak about him in our thinking. The words of both activities come together in one word spoken before the mystery of God: thank you that I am. The Amen spoken in the Eucharist is the word of thanksgiving spoken by the creation to the one who is our beginning and our end, our past and our future, and whose presence is known to us in the words we have spoken to him and about him.

8

The Silence of Thanksgiving

Both prayer and thinking end in silence. That has been the direction of this book: in the end is silence. All the words we speak to God and about him come together in the one word of thanksgiving we speak when in our praying we are able to give thanks for the will that has met us, and when in our thinking we are able to give thanks for the truth that has been shown us. The word of thanksgiving is the final word because it shows us that all our words point us and direct us to their ground in the mystery of God. That word of thanksgiving is a word we shall finally be able to speak only when we and the whole creation are gathered together in offering to the creator, but it is also a word which, in a tentative and partial way, we are able to speak now in the anticipation and hope of being able to speak it finally. We can only speak that word of thanksgiving tentatively and partially now because, as we all know about ourselves, there are still many areas of our lives which are held back from offering, or in which we have not yet allowed the word that God speaks to us to be heard. But, however partially and tentatively the word of thanksgiving may be spoken now, enough is being said for us to continue the journey of our transformation. The Christian hope, however, goes beyond even that journey of our transformation by the Spirit which dwells within us. Our hope goes to the end of the journey—to that hearing of the word of God which is our union with him in silence.

In the centuries of Christian (and non-Christian) speculation about the end of all things in God, many different images have been used to express what our hope is when we say that we believe in the resurrection of the dead and the life of the world to come. All the images which human beings have used have been drawn from our experience of this world, but these images have sought to point us beyond this world to something we have not yet experienced. One of the most vital images in the theological and mystical tradition of Christianity has been that of vision or seeing, of being in the light of God and of seeing into that light. Those who are in the vision of God will see him face-to-face, and in that vision into the depths of God we shall see the unity of all things in their creator. In previous chapters, however, I have begun to develop another image which, while it has its roots in Holy Scripture, has not been as fully developed in the theological or mystical literature of Western Christianity. That image is that of speaking and hearing as they have their end in silence. Certainly it is through speaking and hearing that most of our ordinary relationships with one another come about and grow. We communicate with one another through the spoken and heard word, and in that communication we come to know and love one another. Even more, however, we believe that in the life of Jesus of Nazareth, God spoke his word to us, and we believe that he continues to do so in the word which we receive in the life of the church through preaching and sacrament. Jesus Christ in his life, death, and resurrection is God's word of truth to us. What I hope to do in this final chapter is to develop that image more fully and to suggest that to be in the presence of God, to be united to him, is that silence in which all words we have spoken and heard will be gathered together in the word we shall hear and speak eternally. The Book of Wisdom uses this image when it tells us that in silence the word of God came forth, and we might add that the word which contains all our words returns to God in the silence of eternity.

To think about silence more deeply than we usually do is to begin to see that silence is not just a passive state in which nothing is happening; it is not simply not-speaking but rather an activity, perhaps the most intense activity in which we can engage. Kierkegaard points to the activity of silence when he says that the man of prayer learns that to pray is to hear, to be silent in order that we may hear what is said to us. In a similar way, what happened to Thomas Aquinas toward the end of his life, when he had ceased to speak after speaking so much, points in the same direction. He who had spoken about the mystery of God believed himself to be silent before that mystery. Both these illustrations suggest a great deal about silence that needs to be explored. Because we have seen something of what it is to speak to God and about him, and to hear his word to us, we can now begin to think of silence as our union with God.

In previous chapters, I have used illustrations drawn from our experience of the ordinary relationships we have with one another in order to suggest a way of thinking about our relationship with God in Christ and the Holy Spirit. The significance of such relationships for theology or for the life of prayer is that they draw upon the most profound and serious dimension of human experience; they can show us that the Christian confession of faith always involves a relationship with a God who is deeply personal, one who communicates with us through the word spoken to us, and one with whom we can communicate through our word to him. Such relationships do not exhaust what we believe about our relationship with God, but they do, when we reflect upon them, point beyond themselves to the mystery of our lives as spiritual creatures. But when we begin to think about the final Christian hope of union with God in silence, we are faced with the obvious problem that our hope far exceeds anything we can presently experience and transcends all that we can know or imagine from our life in time and space. Ours is a hope which directs us toward eternity, toward a unity unlike anything we have experienced for ourselves. And yet, because that is our hope, as Christians we need to give ourselves some image through which that hope can be real and significant, and not idle fantasy. To speak of the silence of eternity, as I shall do, requires that the image be grounded in something that we have known, however limited and feeble the image may be.

There are, I believe, two such situations in our experience where something of what that image means can be opened to us. The first is shared at one time or another by most human beings who have ever loved another person. The second, which is a deepening of that experience, Christian people experience more frequently than they might think. Both begin from the words which we speak and which are spoken to us, but both go beyond those words to silence.

From time to time we find ourselves with people whom we love and whom we have known well, who have shared a great deal of our lives with us: parents and children, husbands and wives, very close friends. The experience I mean is what happens when it is no longer necessary to speak, not because there is nothing to be said but because everything has been said and is being said in a different way. What I may be thinking or feeling can be deeply known by another who loves me. That knowledge comes from the words I have spoken in the past, but even more, it comes from the way in which I have presented myself to another in all that I have been. In such a moment of communion with another person, the words I have spoken and the words I do not need to speak are heard in silence. That kind of communion is, in many ways, the most serious and profound kind of communication that we can have with one another, because it arises from the source of all communication which is something more than idle chatter; it arises out of love between human beings. Whenever I try seriously to communicate something of myself to another person, I am speaking and presenting myself out of a communion of love; and whenever I attend seriously to what another person says to me and to how he or she is presented to me, I am attending out of a communion of love. Thus, when the word of love does not need to be spoken in order to be heard, there is a communion which goes more deeply than the spoken word and makes the spoken word possible. Two people who love one another can hear what is not being said, because they attend to one another, they are present to one another. That attending and presence is what I mean by silence. Attending to another person, being present to another, is a deeply personal act beccause it requires an offering of oneself to another. In order to attend to another, I must listen in silence. We know that is true in any serious conversation in which we must be silent in order to hear what is being said. In silent communication the need for attention, listening, is even more important and certainly more difficult because it requires us to turn off even our inner words in order to hear another. In that silence of love, union with another is found.

For most of us, such an experience of silent union is only occasional, for we are usually so busy trying to impress or to move other people through what we say that only occasionally are we able to be silent and thereby to offer ourselves. Certainly that is the case for most of us, even in our thinking and praying. We attend neither to the intelligibility of things nor to the will of God. But in those rare moments when we are silent and do attend to another, we can catch a hint of what union with God means and in what the Christian hope of eternal life is grounded. What we have experienced of God, and what we experience more and more deeply of him as we enter into praying and thinking, is that he is the one who attends to us, who hears us, who presents himself to us in silence.

The second illustration I want to use is drawn particularly from Christian experience, although it has parallels in other religious traditions. It is that which Christians have always called Holy Communion, that act of union with God in Christ which is the central point of the Holy Eucharist. As we have seen in previous chapters, the Holy Eucharist (by whatever name it may be called) has always occupied a central place in the life of the Christian community, because it is in that service of word and action that the church recalls its history and looks forward in hope toward its future in God. The Eucharist is the giving of thanks for God's act of redemption in our history, and so it is the word of thanksgiving. In various signs and images, and in various complex theological formulations, the Christian tradition has sought ways to say that in the word of thanksgiving there is a union between Jesus Christ and the community which believes in him through and in the bread and wine of Holy Communion. The Eucharist is in some way a heightening or a deepening—a completion—of that kind of union of love which we can have in other areas of our lives and which we can only describe through the image of silence. The word of thanksgiving is spoken, and there is the silence of union.

In the New Testament, the image through which the Christian tradition has attempted to express the significance of that silent union with God in Christ is a deeply rich word. That word is *koinonia,* which can be translated as fellowship, sharing, participation, and communion. In the New Testament, *koinonia* is used to express something as simple as sharing alms with those in need, or something as complex and rich as our participation in the life of the Holy Trinity.[1] In each case, there is an intended meaning of union and communion between people, or between people and God, in which they share with one another who and what they are. This sharing is so deep that it can only be described as a participation in one another, an entering into one another, a being with one another. In Holy Communion, as the church has experienced it in the Eucharist, that sharing or being with God in Christ is both the culmination and fulfillment of all forms of human union and communion and the anticipation of that sharing in the life of God himself, which is our hope of eternal life. What is, however, of great significance is that Holy Communion follows upon and completes the word of thanksgiving which the community has declared in word and action. Through the reading and preaching of the word of God and through the prayers, the community has recalled the history of God's saving work and has, in effect, said "Thank you." In that simple act there is a communion with God which draws together all we have spoken to him and about him because all our words are united to the word he there gives to us. It is a silent moment in which we participate in the mystery of God.

These two illustrations of the relationship between the words we speak and silence can, I hope, give intelligibility and greater richness to the few final words I want to say about praying and thinking and how both those activities end in silence. The words are few because we should not speak too much about silence; we should let the images speak for themselves. The end to which we are called by the word of God is that we should be able in every dimension of our being to hear that word and to be united to it so thoroughly that Christ himself becomes and remains our word. When the many words we have spoken throughout our lives—words of love and care, of truth and beauty, as well as words of hatred and scorn, the lies and ugly words—become united in our word of offering and thanksgiving, then we shall know our praying and our thinking for what they truly are. We shall no longer be praying about something or to someone, nor shall we be thinking about something or about someone. We shall be praying with God and thinking with him. In other words, there will be that unity of heart, mind, and will with God that can only be spoken of as love. Then, as Christian faith has always confessed, our humanity, our human word, will participate in the humanity of Jesus who is one with the word of God. "Let this mind be in you which is also in Christ Jesus," Paul says, and under that figure of speech we can hear that to which we are called—silent union in the presence of the mystery of God.

Part Two

MEDITATIONS
ON THE IDOLS
OF OUR TEMPTATION

1

The Idols of Our Temptation

I want to take as a theme for these meditations one which can lead us into an examination of our life as Christians, who have as a sign and guide that cross which shakes and dissolves all our foundations and which shatters all our faith in idols and causes them to come crashing down. I want to think of our temptation and of the way in which the cross of Christ transforms our strength into his glory, and of how it redeems us from the slavery of our idols into his freedom. For this reason, I take as a text the story of the temptation of Christ as it appears in the Gospel of Matthew, in which the time that, according to Mark's Gospel, Jesus spent in the wilderness is given a theological interpretation.

Jesus was then led away by the Spirit into the wilderness, to be tempted by the devil. For forty days and nights he fasted, and at the end of them he was famished. The tempter approached him and said, "If you are the Son of God, tell these stones to become bread." Jesus answered, "Scripture says, 'Man cannot live on bread alone; he lives on every word that God utters.'" The devil then took him to the Holy City and set him on the parapet of the temple. "If you are the Son of God," he said, "throw yourself down; for Scripture says, 'He will put his angels in charge of you, and they will support you in their arms, for fear you should strike your foot against a stone.'" Jesus answered him, "Scripture says again, 'You are not to put the Lord your God to the test.'" Once again, the devil took him to a very high mountain, and showed him all the kingdoms of the world in their glory. "All these," he said, "I will give you, if you will only fall down and do me homage." But Jesus said, "Begone, Satan; Scripture says, 'You shall do homage to the Lord your God and worship him alone.'"

Then the devil left him, and angels appeared and waited on him. [Matt. 4:1–11]

I want to suggest how the temptation of Christ stands as a sign for all of us who are born into him and who bear the image of the cross upon our bodies. To that end, I shall try to suggest first how the cross of Christ shatters every idol by which we would live, and in that shattering enables the Spirit to transform us. For what the cross of Christ must always mean to the Christian is that the idols of our temptation have no power over us, except as we allow them to seduce us by their glitter. It is for the unmasking of the seducer that the cross sheds its light.

The story of the temptation of Jesus has two characteristics that I hope we shall keep in mind as we make our way, for I shall return to them from time to time. In all three synoptic Gospels, the story of the temptation comes after the baptism of Jesus by John. What, of course, that baptism signifies is the beginning of Jesus' messianic calling. Jesus undertook to do the work that was set before him. He went into Galilee and began his public ministry. Thus, the three temptations must be seen in terms of his calling and his beginning. The devil tempted him precisely at that point where he had come to begin what he was called to do, even though he may not yet have known to what end he was called.

For anyone who is about to begin an important work, the time of beginning is always a most vulnerable time, for it is a time when we know that we are called to something, but we do not yet know the end of that calling. But we should miss the point of the temptation of Jesus were we not also to see that it is the temptation of the Christian that is involved here. The Christian always stands at the point of beginning and at the point of calling. That is what our baptism has done to us. The calling of Jesus is the call to do the will of his Father, and that will leads to the cross. That is, as we know, always the Christian calling. It is at the point of our beginning—where each of us is—that temptation comes to us. Our temptation begins at the point of our calling, just as it did for Jesus. And as we are always called to begin, so we are always tempted.

All this suggests a second thing about the temptation of Jesus that we must keep in mind as we go along. All the synoptic Gospels agree that Jesus was led into the wilderness by the Spirit. His going was not something he sought but something to which he was led. He who later in his ministry taught us to pray "Lead us not into temptation" was himself led into temptation. There is a great mystery here—a paradox if you will—which no exegete or theologian I know of has ever been able to solve to any degree of satisfaction. Temptation is never that which we seek, because what we seek ultimately has no power over us. Temptation is always something into which we are led, and that into which we are led has power over us, a power that can destroy us or deliver us. The God we seek is always an idol; the God who leads us is our redeemer. So, when we consider temptation—whether of Jesus or of ourselves—we are considering that fine point of distinction between destruction and salvation, idolatry and worship, slavery and freedom. The distinction is very fine, and it is not until we are delivered from evil that we can know who has led us into temptation. The cross made clear to Jesus who had led him into temptation. May that same cross make clear to us who leads us into temptation.

2

The Idol of Need

For forty days and nights he fasted, and at the end of them he
was famished. The tempter approached him and said, "If you
are the Son of God, tell these stones to become bread." [Matt.
4:2–3]

We are considering the idols of our temptation—those idols
to which we are led and which, if we fall down and worship
them, have the power to destroy us. Into what idol of temptation is Jesus here led?

The text is very clear. At the conclusion of his fasting, shortly
after his baptism by John, the tempter says to him, "If you are
the Son of God, if you believe that God has chosen and called
you, if you believe that you are what many will say you are, then
satisfy your need. You have fasted long and you are famished,
so take these ordinary stones and turn them into bread for yourself." And, of course, he could do so. He who had the power to
turn water into wine, to feed the thousands, to heal the sick, he
could turn stones into bread. To do so was such a small thing to
do, of no great moment, affecting no one else because no one
else need know what had happened to the stones. The act would
be between the tempter and himself. He could satisfy his own
need and be filled.

If he had, that would have been the end of the matter. The
idol would have been set up and worshiped—the idol of his own
need. For Jesus was hungry. He was hungry for bread after his
fasting, but he was hungry also to begin his work or as he was to
say later, to do the will of his Father.

What a strange and familiar temptation that is. We who are
at the beginning of our calling and who are hungry to do God's

will can catch a glimpse of what is happening to our Lord here in the wilderness. For we who struggle with our hunger know, at least dimly, that fine line between a need to do God's work and a need to do our own. And the focal point of that struggle—of that temptation—is our need, our very human and ordinary hunger.

For temptation, when we first meet it and always thereafter, tempts us as it did Jesus at the very place where we are most human: at that point where we stand in need, where we are hungry. That need is our humanity, our creatureliness and our fragility. We do need so many things simply to keep on going. We need food and clothing, affection and love from others, some recognition and signs of success for our efforts. Without these things we should die, for we are creatures who stand always in need.

And that, of course, is the point where the idol of our temptation can be set up. "Turn these stones into bread. You are hungry; your need is right and just; you are, after all, human, a fragile vessel. No one will know; feed that need." But the tempter is very subtle. The idol is not simply that which satisfies our need; that would be an idol of our own making, and we should soon see through it, for the flesh that is satiated soon knows better. No, the temptation into which we are led, the idol which calls for our worship, is the need itself. The idol that can destroy us is our hunger, not the bread which satisfies our hunger. The tempter, who was more subtle than any beast of the field, said to Jesus, "Feed on your own need. Live on it. Turn those stones into bread and be filled with yourself." And, of course, we—like Jesus—can do just that, for it is not the satisfaction but the need itself that is either our glory or our condemnation. The cross stands at that subtle point of our temptation as the tree stood in the middle of the Garden of Eden. Our father Adam took and ate. Jesus says to the tempter: "Scripture says, 'Man cannot live on bread alone; he lives on every word that God utters.'"

3

The Idol of Testing

The devil then took him to the Holy City and set him on the parapet of the temple. "If you are the Son of God," he said, "throw yourself down; for Scripture says, 'He will put his angels in charge of you, and they will support you in their arms, for fear you should strike your foot against a stone.'" [Matt. 4:5-6]

We have considered the first temptation of Jesus as the idol of his and our need, that idol which is not our bread but our hunger. When Jesus refused to worship that idol, he was taken to the Holy City and set on the parapet of the temple. The first temptation was a private affair between Jesus and the tempter, now his temptation becomes public, for the idol can be set up in the very temple of God. He who later was able to speak of his own body as the temple was himself tempted in the midst of the temple.

The tempter begins again in the same manner: "If you are the Son of God, then cast yourself down and your Father will take care of you. If you are the Son of God, God will not let any evil happen to you." Once again the tempter showed his subtlety, for he quoted to Jesus from one of the Psalms in order to prove to him that he did not need to fear. The Psalm speaks of trust in the Lord. "You live under God's care; therefore do not fear, for your God is a safe refuge." The Psalm speaks of hope in God, but the tempter tried to turn that hope to fear and despair, for he said to Jesus, "If you are the Son of God, then put God to the test." The Psalm says that when we are put to the test we should trust in God. The tempter said, "Put God to the test and see if he will save you."

What a subtle temptation that was for Jesus here at the begin-ning, for he would have to deal with it throughout his ministry. Whenever he healed the sick or stilled the waters, or, most im-portant of all, when he began that final journey to the cross, that temptation would be there: "If I am your Son, your chosen one, then heal this person; do what I ask, take this cross from me. Do not put me to the test; let me put you to the test."

We can hear ourselves in that temptation, for we know in how many ways we put one another and God and even ourselves to the test. "If you love me, do what I want. If you are to be my friend, become what I want you to be." We say all those things to one another. And what is it we say to God? "If you want me to do your will, then make the way straight and easy. If you want me to be pure, then take away all my desires. If you want me to be a good person, then make all my problems clear and unambiguous. If you want me to believe, show me a sign." Our lives with one another and with God are filled with so many conditional clauses. The tempter is very subtle; he goes to the heart of the matter: If . . . then . . . !

But again we must ask what idol it is that tempts us here. Clearly it is not the idol of getting our own way, for most of us learn rather quickly that we usually do not get our own way. That idol would not deceive us for long. The temptation is in the testing, whether it be of another or of God, and the idol that is set up to be worshiped is that of our own despair. Over and over the people asked Jesus for a sign in order that he might prove himself, but the response that ran through all his teaching was the same: "Even if one rose from the dead you would not believe." The temptation to ask for a sign, for proof, is the idol of despair. Once we begin to test another, there is no end to our testing. The demand for a sign always carries with it the doubt and fear that even the sign is not to be trusted, for no sign can be trusted against an unknown future. To demand such a sign is to demand to know what my future will be, to demand to know what will be my good and my evil. And that demand, in what-ever form it may come, can lead to only one end—to despair—for there is only One who knows what will be our good. To believe that we can know what will be our good or our evil is to demand to be God, and that is to die in the act of worshiping the idol of our own despair.

Eve said to the tempter, "We may eat of any tree in the Garden except for the tree in the middle of the Garden; God has forbidden us either to eat or to touch the fruit of that tree; if we do we shall die." But the serpent said, "Of course you will not die. God knows that as soon as you eat it, your eyes will be opened and you will be like gods, knowing both good and evil."

Now the cross stands in the middle of the garden of Eden as the sign of our hope. And he, who did not think equality with God a thing to be grasped, he who is now the temple of God, said to the tempter, "Scripture says again, 'You are not to put the Lord your God to the test.'"

4

The Idol of Worship

Once again, the devil took him to a very high mountain, and showed him all the kingdoms of the world in their glory. "All these," he said, "I will give you, if you will only fall down and do me homage." [Matt. 4:8–9]

We have seen how the tempter presented to Jesus the idols of his need and despair as idols before which he could worship himself. In each of those temptations, the tempter began by calling attention to who Jesus is: "If you are the Son of God, then do this." Jesus, in all the weakness of his own humanity, was being tempted to worship himself. Even the settings for those temptations are important, for the first was a private affair between Jesus and the tempter, and the second was on Jesus' home ground, so to speak, for Jesus was being tempted to give a sign to a people who were always demanding such a sign and who—if the sign were convincing enough—would believe in him for a time, at least until someone more interesting came along. And that, of course, is always the end of those who make themselves their own idol. There will always be someone better at it who can set up a more powerful idol. Had Jesus worshiped the idol of himself, he would soon have been found out and replaced.

The cross shattered both those temptations, and Jesus was led to a new place and a new temptation. The tempter no longer quoted Scripture; he no longer appealed to Jesus' sonship, nor did he offer Jesus people to rule as a god. Instead, he took Jesus to a mountain (one might wonder if it was the same mountain on which he was later transfigured) and offered him all the kingdoms of the world. "If you will worship me," Satan says,

97

"all this is yours." To worship the tempter! Now it was all out in the open! Jesus was offered power in return for worshiping the one who could give him power. He who had the power to cast out demons, to rule the sea, to raise the dead, to forgive sins—was being offered power over all the powers there are except for one. And that, of course, was the hitch. He had to worship the one who gives him such power. He would receive power by placing himself in the power of another.

Power, as we know, is a very funny kind of thing. All of us know to some degree what it is like to have power over another person or to be in the power of someone else. We know, or at least we shall learn, that the power to do good can easily become the power to do evil. And that is a problem with which we must live and struggle, for power is a reality of life that cannot be avoided. And, as we have seen, we are always led into the temptation of our strength, not of our weakness.

But there is more to the matter than that. The danger is not in our power itself but in what we worship as the source of our power. The idol which can destroy us is the one from which we receive our power.

What I wish to point to here is what I believe to be the mystery at the deep center of our spirituality: that sin of Adam from which all our sins derive. Jesus had seen through himself. Now he had to see through the tempter, and that is very difficult to do, for the tempter may well be the God who led him into the wilderness and who was now tempting him. Can we, perhaps, without being too flagrant in our interpretation, imagine the tempter saying to Jesus, "You believe in God as the source of all power and might, but which God?" I think we may imagine that, because most of us have heard that voice ourselves. We believe in God, certainly, because we are not fools, but which God? Which God gives you power and asks only for your worship in return?

I cannot answer that question for anyone else, because each of us must work out his or her own answer. Nor can I here answer it for myself, because I do not yet know how. But I do think we can say what answer Jesus himself gave, and that is much more important for us, because that is why he is our savior. He gave an answer in both word and deed. He said to the tempter, "You shall do homage to the Lord your God and worship him alone." And, having said that, he began the way of the cross on which every idol was shattered for him and for us. Matthew's Gospel tells us that at his crucifixion Jesus was derided for trusting in God and that when he had breathed his last the curtain of the temple was torn in two from top to bottom. There was an earthquake; the rocks split, and the graves opened. The God who shatters even the idol that we would make him to be, is the one whom Jesus worshiped on the cross, and for that reason we can say that it is the faithful cross, the one and only noble tree, our only hope.

5

The God of Faith

Jesus answered: "Scripture says, 'Man cannot live on bread alone; he lives on every word that God utters.'" [Matt. 4:4]

We have been thinking about the temptations of Jesus at the outset of his ministry. Now we must begin to think about the transformation of those temptations at the end when all the foundations have been shaken and all the idols have been thrown down. We must begin to think of that end which is our beginning and our new creation.

The first idol that Jesus destroys is the idol of his and our need. Adam, when he was tempted, took and ate. Jesus, when he was tempted, said, "Man cannot live on bread alone; he lives on every word that God utters."

The ministry of Jesus was prefigured in that response. Indeed, it became a major theme in everything that he did and in everything that has been said about him. Jesus fed the multitudes in the wilderness as his Father fed his people long before, and he taught his disciples to pray, "Give us this day our daily bread." John, meditating on the mystery of Christ, calls him the bread of life, that true bread which comes down from heaven, that living water which quenches all thirst. And it is on the feast of Unleavened Bread that Jesus sat with his disciples at supper and there took bread and said, "This is my body." He can do that, of course, because the idol of his need was cast down. The bread that Jesus would not make for himself, he now becomes for us. His need became transformed into his gift, and it became that by which we live, for just as it is the idol to which we are led, not that which we make for ourselves which can destroy us, so the bread that transforms us is the bread we are given and not the bread we would make for ourselves. The reason for that is clear. The bread of life we are given feeds not our need but our faith; it transforms our need into faith. To eat that bread which Jesus gives and which he says is his body is to live not by our need but by faith.

The subtlety of the tempter is to make us think that we can satisfy our need, and so, when Adam was deceived by the tempter and was cast from the garden, God said to him, "With labor shall you earn your food all the days of your life . . . you shall gain your bread by the sweat of your brow." And so indeed we do. But now the cross stands in the middle of the garden, and the subtlety of God—who is even more subtle than the tempter, for he is a consuming fire—is to teach us in our need what it is to receive. To receive the free gift that is given there on the cross, to eat of that bread, is faith, and that requires more of us than the sweat of our brow. It requires of us the discipline of the cross.

How easy it is to receive a gift! The gift of love that another person gives us—nothing could be easier than to be loved by someone. Or the gift of forgiveness—nothing could be easier than to be forgiven after we have been stupid and wrong. Or the gift of a vocation—nothing could be easier than doing God's work.

So we always think at the beginning, when first we are tempted by God or by the tempter. And then we learn what it is that is required of those who have received such a gift, or else we turn back into ourselves and to our idol. The discipline of the cross is the discipline of learning to receive the gift that is given without turning it into that which satisfies our need. For to believe that the point of the gift is to satisfy our need is to turn stones into bread, but into bread which will always leave us more hungry in our need.

What the subtle God requires of us in the discipline of the cross is that we should learn to receive the gift, not for our need but only because the gift is given. That is to live by faith and not by need.

As on that last night with his disciples he took bread and blessed it, Jesus stood between his temptation in the wilderness and the cross outside the city. In standing there, he gives us the bread of life. And we, as we receive it, stand between that same temptation and that same cross. In receiving that bread, we learn what it is to say, "Man cannot live on bread alone; he lives on every word that God utters"—for in receiving him, we receive the one who is the bread of Life and the word of Life, the one who gives himself upon the tree.

6

The God of Hope

Jesus answered him, "Scripture says again, 'You are not to put the Lord your God to the test.'" [Matt. 4:7]

In our consideration of the temptations of Jesus and their transformation in the cross, we have stood with our Lord between his temptation in the wilderness and the cross outside the city, and we have seen how the idol of his need was transformed into that faith which made it possible for him to become the bread by which we are fed. Now we have moved to that cross outside the city and we stand with him at the cross and look toward the day of the resurrection—the eighth day as the fathers called it, because it is the day of the new creation. Faith has brought Jesus to the place where he now is, as indeed it brings us there. Faith has brought him to the cross, for the discipline of the cross requires of him and of us that we learn to receive the gift that is given. Faith in God—or even, as we sometimes learn, faith in another person—brings us to the point where nothing is left but hope. That idol which is our despair is that we should become as gods and know good and evil; our hope is God's promise in his Son.

But the way from the place where he is able to feed us with the bread of life to the place where he becomes our hope is not an easy way, either for him or for us. For our Lord, it was a way that led him through the despair of his betrayal by one whom he had chosen, through the agony of doubt in the Garden, when he prayed that the cup might be taken from him, through his being deserted and abandoned by those whom he loved, through the knowledge that all he had worked for had come to naught, and finally to the cross and death itself. We can, if we will listen, hear the depth of that despair in the words "My God, my God, why hast thou forsaken me?" It is to that point of nakedness before the God who had brought him there, and before those who surrounded the cross and who could say, "He saved others, but he cannot save himself," that his faith has led him, for after he had resisted the second temptation of the tempter, Jesus could never make his obedience conditional upon anything. He could not put his Father to the test; he had no way of testing or knowing or controlling what his future might be. The tempter, when he deceived our first parents, told them they would not have to die. Now Jesus had before him only death, and that death is our hope.

How easy it is for us to be deceived about hope. What we want to do is to believe that God will work out everything for our good in the end. The way may be difficult; things may get bad at times, but in the end all will be well. And sometimes, indeed, it does happen that way, and we are deceived all the more. We even try to do it with Jesus himself. We interpret his death according to our own understanding and our own idols: God made it all right for him, so he will make it all right for us. And so we avoid the cross and what it says, for it is not too difficult to turn the cross itself into that which puts God to the test. "I am your son, your chosen one, surely you are not going to abandon me now." We can imagine that Jesus might have said that, might perhaps have thought it, because we have said it so many times ourselves.

But Jesus had shattered that idol long ago; he does not worship it upon the cross, nor will the cross allow us to worship it. The cross frees us from that temptation, and that is our only hope. The cross is set in the middle of the garden, and it frees us from the sin of testing, which is our despair. The cross frees us from the sin of testing, because Jesus died there; it is the end. Nothing is left, nothing on which he or we can depend except the cross, and the cross offers us nothing, not even itself. It offers only the God who led Jesus there and who leads us there to be crucified with him.

Because we have not yet gone the final way, we are not yet able to understand the cross or to understand the hope it offers us by taking every ground of hope away from us. The cross stands there at the beginning and at the end of all the days we have known and in which we still live. We look back to the cross as we look back to Jesus who died on it. And that looking back is dark and difficult because whatever meaning it may have for us is still obscured by the meaning we would give it. We have not yet cast down the idols of our need and of our despair. And yet, in our looking back to the cross, it stands before us still in darkness, for we have not yet died there with Christ, but with a darkness of light, with that luminous darkness which is the promise of God, our only hope, the eighth day of the Creation.

7

The God of Love

Jesus said, "Begone, Satan; Scripture says, 'You shall do homage to the Lord your God and worship him alone.'" Then the devil left him, and angels appeared and waited on him. [Matt. 4:10–11]

We have stood at the cross where Jesus dies in the darkness. That cross and that dying are always in the darkness for us, for they speak of our sins, our blindness and confusion. But now as we stand there in the darkness of the cross—for there is no other place where we can stand—we look beyond it to a light which shines in the darkness: to the day of resurrection. For Jesus the last idol has been cast down; he was raised from the dead.

In considering the last temptation of Jesus in the wilderness, I suggested that it was only after Jesus had seen through himself, through the idol of his need and the idol of his despair, that he could face that final idol, the tempter himself. Only as Jesus' need was transformed into faith, and as despair was transformed into hope, could the final idolatry of power be transformed into love. On the cross, Jesus knew which God had tempted him and transformed him in order that he might worship him alone. He knew that the source of his power was the God who is love.

We say so easily that God is love, and we say even more easily that we love one another. And, of course, it is right that we should love one another, for in the beginning there is nothing easier than to say "I love you," and at the end there is nothing easier than to say "I love you." It is between the beginning and the end that we discover how difficult it is to speak of love. For Jesus and for us, to speak of love is the way of the cross in faith and hope. At the end of that way he was raised from the dead, and he shows us the God who is love.

If we consider ourselves, perhaps we can see what is happening here a bit more clearly. Love is power, the power of another, and it can lead either to the idolatry of ourselves (that sin of Adam which is called pride and concupiscence) or to worship. That is why love is always a dark night, for in it we are called to receive a gift that is given to us—for love is always a gift, never something we have deserved—just as we are called to forgo every testing of good and evil and to live only in the promise that is given. To love another is to be in darkness, because we do not know from where it has come or to what it will lead. To love another tempts us at that fine point which is the difference between life and death, between faith and need, between hope and despair.

And once again the cross stands in the middle of the garden, which love indeed is. For it is the cross that transforms the darkness of our sin into the light of Christ. Because of the cross the darkness shines with the presence of the God who is light, who has now fully shown himself in our darkness.

On the eve of the resurrection the church sings of that holy and blessed night in which the children of Israel were led from bondage, in which Christ broke the bonds of death and hell, in which heaven and earth are joined and humankind is reconciled to God. This indeed is what the resurrection of Jesus is: the light of God's victory in our dark night.

To stand at the foot of the cross, as we still do, is to look into the light of God, which is love. To look into the light of God is to meet the risen Lord, and that is neither to understand nor to test, neither to grasp nor to prove, but simply to know who our God is and to love him. That is our beginning and our end. The resurrection is for Jesus the end of the way of the cross. The devil has left him, and angels minister to him. For us it is still our beginning, our end which is yet to be. Because of the love by which it tempts us, we set forth upon the way of the cross, and we are led by the Spirit into the wilderness, where we are fed by the bread of life. Because of the power the way of the cross gives us, we believe it will bring us and all God's people to that vision and to that city where we shall know what we love and love what we know and live in that light—to whom be ascribed all might, majesty, power, and dominion, henceforth and to all ages.

Notes

CHAPTER 1

1. Josef Pieper, *The Silence of St. Thomas* (New York: Christian Classics, 1957), p. 38.

2. Søren Kierkegaard, "The Lilies of the Field and the Birds of the Air," in *Christian Discourses,* trans. Walter Lowrie (Princeton: Princeton University Press, 1940), p. 323.

CHAPTER 2

1. Dietrich Bonhoeffer, *Creation and Fall,* trans. John C. Fletcher (New York: Macmillan, 1959), p. 72.

2. In *Theology of the Sacraments* (New York: Scribner, 1957), pp. 47–52, Donald M. Baillie points out that the best contemporary translation of *pneumatikos* would be "personal," and the best translation for *sarkikos* would be "not to live in personal relationships." As he says, in the New Testament this distinction does not suggest an opposition between the spiritual and the body or the natural, and it certainly does not suggest the contemporary meaning of flesh as the dimension of sexual desire.

3. This is attributed to Athanasius, *De incarnatione et contra Arianos,* 8, as cited in J. N. D. Kelly, *Early Christian Doctrines* (New York: Harper & Row, 1978), p. 352.

4. Cyprian *De catholicae ecclesiae unitate* 6, 7.

CHAPTER 3

1. Paul Tillich, *Systematic Theology* (Chicago: University of Chicago Press, 1951), 1:170. Tillich's discussion of "the word as a medium of revelation and the question of the inner word," pp. 122–126, is illuminating and helpful. He says, for example, "Language as a medium of revelation . . . has the 'sound' and 'voice' of the divine mystery in and through the sound and voice of human

expression and denotation. Language with this power is the 'Word of God'" (p. 124).

2. Bernard Lonergan, *Insight* (New York: Philosophical Library, 1970), p. 348. The "pure desire to know" is fundamental to Lonergan's approach to theology; it parallels such ideas as transcendental openness in the theology of Karl Rahner. See most especially his *Foundations of Christian Faith* (New York: Seabury Press, 1978).

3. The two quotations from Thomas Aquinas are cited in Pieper, *The Silence of St. Thomas*, p. 55. They are taken from Aquinas's commentary on 1 Tim. 6:4 and the commentary on the *Liber de Causis 1.6*.

4. In his commentary on Psalms 36 and 43, Augustine develops the image of Christ as the Light. See *Select Library of the Nicene and Post Nicene Fathers of the Christian Church*, First Series, ed. Philip Schaff (New York, 1888), 8:89–90, 139.

5. Augustine *De trinitate* 1.6.

6. Gregory of Nyssa *The Life of Moses* 376C–377A. Cited in Jean Daniélou, ed., "Entering the Dark Cloud," in *From Glory to Glory: Texts from Gregory of Nyssa's Mystical Writings*, trans. and ed. Herbert Musurillo (New York: Scribner, 1961), p. 118.

CHAPTER 5

1. The image comes from Thomas Aquinas's discussion of the necessity of grace for beatitude. He argues that God is prepared to give grace to all human beings, "but those alone are deprived of grace, who place in themselves an obstacle to grace: thus he who shuts his eyes while the sun is shining is to be blamed if an accident occurs, although he is unable to see unless the sun's light enable him to do so." *Summa Contra Gentiles* 3.159. A similar imagery is used in "Treatise on Grace" in the *Summa Theologiae*, pt. 1a2ae, quest. 109, arts. 1 and 6.

CHAPTER 8

1. *Koinonia* as sharing with others in their need is used primarily in Rom. 12:13; 15:26; Phil. 4:15. It has also the sense of sharing in the mystery of Christ and of the Trinity in 1 John 1:3; 6:7; 1 Pet. 5:1. It is also the word used by Paul when he speaks of our sharing in the body and blood of Christ (1 Cor. 10:14–17).